What's the difference between saints, heroes, other great achievers — and the rest of us? Not their natural gifts, but their *acquired* ability to focus their wills toward high aims, writes the distinguished psychologist (of the old school) Jesuit Johann Lindworsky.

A pioneer in the psychology of the will, Fr. Lindworsky penned many scholarly works, but nothing for the average layman until this popular book, designed to put his findings to practical use.

But he had a second, vital purpose: to counteract dangerous writings in psychology that were luring Catholics into error. Grounded in sound science *and* Catholic principles, Fr. Lindworsky's wisdom is as timeless and effective as most modern "self-help" books are faddish and misleading.

Catholic reviewers hailed the original 1929 edition:

> "In the flood of current behavioristic literature with its total disregard or outright denial of the existence of the will, it is refreshing to come upon a work treating specifically of this largely neglected subject. When it is discussed by a master such as the distinguished Jesuit psychologist, Father Lindworsky, it becomes a matter of importance in the literature of education and psychology." — *Commonweal*

> "Parents, teachers and others who have to deal with guiding and strengthening the wills of the young will especially profit." — *America*

THE TRAINING OF THE WILL

JOHANN LINDWORSKY, S.J.

THE TRAINING OF THE WILL

TRANSLATED BY

A. STEINER

AND

E. A. FITZPATRICK

ROMAN CATHOLIC BOOKS
P.O. Box 2286
Ft. Collins, CO 80522-2286

Nihil obstat: H. B. Ries, Censor librorum
Imprimatur: ✠ S. G. Messmer, Archiepiscopus Milwaukiensis
July 29, 1929

This edition first published in 1932

ISBN 0-912141-31-X

FROM THE PREFACE OF THE FIRST EDITION

AFTER repeated requests of the editor of this series, I have put on paper and enlarged, from the pedagogical viewpoint, the lectures on the psychology and pedagogy of the will, which I delivered at educational conferences at Arnsberg, Dortmund, and elsewhere. Intended in the first place for study groups of practice teachers, the book might prove useful also to larger circles.

The problems compiled in the third part are intended for study groups. Each problem in this part must be preceded by a careful report on the corresponding sections of the first and second part, independent of the presentation in the book. Although the problems in the third part are very concise in their wordings, they require not a little preparation. The applications which are found among the problems concerning self-education should remind the young practice teachers that all educational demands made on the pupil presuppose similar demands on the educator.

Unlike the other volumes of the series, no references to collateral literature are given here. Independent thinking and acting are more important in our field than extensive readings. Access to the psychological literature on this subject is offered by the author's book entitled *The Will* (3rd ed., 1923); the reader will find references to further questions of life in general in the splendid work of Privy Councilor Fassbender's *Wollen, eine königliche Kunst* (Volition, a Royal Art, 10th ed., 1920). C. Gutberlet has written excellently on the freedom of the will in *Die Willensfreiheit und ihre Gegner* – "The Freedom of Will and Its Opponents" (2nd ed., 1907).

J. LINDWORSKY, S.J.

Cologne, May, 1922

PREFACE OF THE FOURTH EDITION

The scientific forerunner of this book was a critical study of the research in the field of the psychology of the will, including the experiments up to 1910. Addressed to a limited professional group, it appeared as a separate book under the title of "The Will, Its Manifestations and Control According to the Results of Experimental Research" (Leipzig-Barth, 1919, 3rd ed., 1923). As an outcome of this work, the author was called upon to lecture on the subject before groups of educators, and was asked to write out his addresses in the form of the present book. The third edition was somewhat expanded to incorporate suggestions received by the author.

Prague, 1932

CONTENTS

INTRODUCTION

The Practical Importance of the Will. The art of willing has interested the mind in all ages. Will, it appears, has made every great man what he is. Wealth, strength, health, even intellectual endowments seem to be more or less replaceable by exceptional will power. We read how Demosthenes, in spite of his feeble voice, his unfavorable appearance, and his initial failure, by sheer will power trained himself to become the first orator of Greece. When we learn how many a general of the past, though frail of body and even ill, won the most glorious of battles, when we observe how many a businessman, beginning with empty hands, has worked himself up to become a captain of finance, we may be indifferent to the ideals which impelled them, we may even detest these ideals, but we are thrilled by the accomplishments and should like, in another sphere perhaps, to achieve similar success. We have always been told, and it is confirmed by experience that if we will, nothing is impossible; but we must be able to will. That is why so many books on the art of willing have enjoyed great popularity. That is why we lend a ready ear to everyone who promises to help us acquire an energetic will.

Will Training, if Possible, Most Urgent Duty of School. If the training of the will is possible, then this training must be the duty, nay even the most urgent duty, of the school. If it is possible to cultivate the will through personal activity, then this personal activity must claim the first place in the course of training. If it is possible to strengthen our own will, then this endeavor must precede all other interests of our private life. But how should we train our will?

New Points of View in Training the Will. A considerable number of volumes on the training of the will are available, and a new book on this subject may, therefore, appear superfluous. I should indeed not have attempted to write the present book, if I did not believe that I can say something different from what has been said. For recent findings of experimental research on the will are to be considered in this book in detail and are to furnish new points of view. The present monograph promises, accordingly, to present something novel on the training of the will. The novelty of it will prove quite striking. I must admit in advance that I am not able to point out an altogether simple means of training the will. Furthermore, I cannot assert that success will result from the application of my method as naturally as a cure results from the use of a medicine. I am stating the matter more correctly if I say that my means are infallible, but that I cannot just hand them over to you. I can only say: Here, beneath this surface rock, gold is hidden; dig for it, doing your level best, and you shall surely find all you need for your life. If, however, you wish to become a great man among those who will, a kindly genius must guide your hand so that you begin digging at the right spot and find a very rich vein.

Many False Conceptions of the Will. The results of experimental psychology indicate clearly that there are many false conceptions of the nature and function of the will. These partly erroneous conceptions must be blamed for the fact that many of the systems of will training lack unity; many are uncertain, some are ineffective, a few even questionable. If it were possible to ask those who have attended some of the famous training schools of the will, how much they have profited by their earnest study, the answers would not be very encouraging. If I went so far as to ask these persons whether they became stronger in the weakest point of their moral life, I should probably receive most crushing replies. At the same time, there will be found a small number of people who can speak of genuine and lasting success. We shall not question their assertions, but we will point out later, in detail, that some of the highly praised means of training the will are to an extent accidental successes. As most trainers of the will, who advertise their wares, have no scientific and unified conception of the will, they are often at a loss to know just what constitutes the efficiency of their methods and devices. Thus, they direct the attention of their students to the shell, and, as a consequence, most of their pupils reach for the shell. A few, however, luckier than the rest, accidentally gain possession of the kernel with the shell, seize the essence of will training with the superficial, and these succeed.

Psychology at the Basis of the Pedagogy of Will. With the foregoing in mind, it will be apparent that we cannot avoid discussing in detail the psychology of the will before we speak of the training of the will. We shall confine ourselves, however, to strictly necessary matters, and explain them in popular language, even though the scientific phenomena involved may not always be described in the most accurate way. Quite necessarily we shall omit all but a limited number of scientific proofs. Those who wish to inform themselves more thoroughly on the subject are referred to the writer's book, *Der Wille,* fourth edition. The present outline must not be regarded as a substitute for the extended study of fundamental principles discussed in this larger work. However, every significant principle for everyday work is here presented. The reader is cautioned not to shun the basic theory of the subject; otherwise the practical applications which will be suggested will fail in inner clarity, and the reader will lack a sure foundation of principles for practical use.

I

THE PSYCHOLOGY OF WILL

THE ACT OF WILL

THE fundamental question antecedent to any attempt at training the will is: *Is there a will?* Let us see. No one has ever doubted the fact that there are certain specific happenings in human life, commonly called "acts of will." If I decide to write a letter, and have made this decision after a painstaking effort which I finally convert into action, no one will question that we are dealing here with inner happenings. These happenings can neither be called perception, nor thinking, nor feeling, but are of such a nature as to form, in contradistinction to other intellectual experiences, a category of their own: *acts of the will.* An experience such as this, however, is no simple act, but a most complex phenomenon. Perception, thinking, feeling, remembering, and many other elements enter into it. Therefore, the question is justified whether or not such a decision could perhaps be explained from a combination of the well-known acts of thinking, perceiving, and feeling alone, or if analysis leads us to find a new act, distinct from all the others; that is to say, the act of will.

Common Sense by Introspection Affirms a Distinct Act of Will. Common sense has never doubted that there is a peculiar inner experience in addition to thinking, feeling, and external acting which, even prior to philosophic speculation, had received a special name. Everybody who is not yet prejudiced by a philosophical theory is thoroughly convinced of the existence of the act of will. Even as late as thirty years ago, experimental psychologists would have attached little importance to this general conviction of mankind. Indeed, the fact that psychology could dispense with ordinary introspection was regarded as a great step forward. Meanwhile, experimental psychology as a result of increasing experimentation has done justice to introspection, practically as well as theoretically. Today we know that deliberate and simultaneous, as well as subsequent introspection, performed as a result of theoretical interest, is not an altogether unobjectionable scientific source of knowledge; however we know, too, that retrospective introspection, done immediately after an experience without the prejudice of a preconceived theory, is perfectly reliable. For, our experiences do not disappear at once into the realm of the unconscious, but fade away gradually. We can look back to these receding processes retrospectively and, without altering or influencing them, catch some of their features. We often practice this retrospection in everyday life, actuated by practical motives rather than by a theoretical psychological interest. "Just what was it?" "How in the world did it happen?" "Was I at fault?" – we ask such questions often immediately after inner processes which we observe without any theoretical prepossession. Therefore, if countless millions of untrained observers arrive at the conviction of having experienced a peculiar process which appears to them as something very simple and distinct from all thinking, imagining, feeling, and acting, this general conviction is entitled to a purely scientific evaluation.

Will Rejected by Philosophical Theory. That is why sound philosophy adhered to this conviction until the time of the English skeptics. These began questioning the act of will as a real and distinct elementary experience not on the basis of experience, but because it conflicted with other philosophical theories. The will did not fit at all into a conception which wished to explain the concepts of substance and causality in terms of subjective delusions. Since these attempts at explanation originated, in their turn, in the tendency to break with the traditional conception of the soul, Hume's doctrine of will and that of his followers cannot be considered as having been arrived at without bias. When, about the middle of the past century, experimental psychology arose in Germany, most of its proponents embraced English sensism. They did so partly on account of the prevailing scientific materialistic trend of the age, and partly because English sensism, with its stress on the doctrine of association, seemed to offer the most convenient and methodically the clearest approach to scientific research of the spiritual processes. Hence, most experimental psychologists originally rejected the will as an elementary experience beyond sensation and feeling.

Experimental Research at First Rejects the Will. In the beginning, this denial of the will was not based on experimental findings. And when experimental research on the act of the will began, the first experimental findings justified the empirical point of view. With the observations in the field of physics in mind, it was held that in psychological experimentation the simplest processes should be examined first. The person who was experimented upon had, for example, to press an electrical key at the moment he perceived a certain color. The act of pressing the key happened, however, also when the person who was experimented upon reacted without any conscious participation. No trace of the act of will was to be discovered in that; thus, a so-called voluntary action appeared to be possible without an act of will. Later, it was discovered that almost all concepts, but especially the concepts of movements, were accompanied by very slight movements of the hands, the head, the skin of the forehead, etc. The persons experimented upon knew nothing of such movements; in fact, denied them most decidedly. Accordingly, the mystery of the action of the will appeared to be solved. The percepts, even without any act of will, produced movements, and the action flowed directly from the percepts. The difference between these so-called involuntary and voluntary movements and actions consisted merely in the fact that in the case of the former the aim to be achieved had not been thought of; whereas in the latter the aim had been imagined in advance. Accordingly, the picturing (*Vorstellung*) of the aim to be achieved was the decisive element determining the acts of will. Of course, critical minds were not satisfied with this theory for reasons which remain to be discussed. Still, for the time being, this theory represented the finding of experimental research until the experimental method had made twofold progress.

Systematic Experimental Introspection Admitted. Introspection, which in the beginning of the experimental period had been completely banished from psychological research, returned by the very road of experimentation.

It was noticed, after some time, that the simplest psychological experiments could lead to totally different results even if the external conditions of the experiment were kept alike with scrupulous accuracy. The inner attitude of the person experimented upon could vary greatly, and the outcome of the experiments depended far more upon his inner attitude than on the external conditions. And yet, only the subject of the experiment could speak of his inner attitude. Thus, introspection could not be dispensed with. Nevertheless, psychology did not simply return to the position held before Fechner. As already stated, no scientific significance can be attributed to every act of introspection, but practically only to that form of retrospective and unbiased introspection which is secured most readily by means of experiments. It is a peculiarity of all psychological experiments that they require two subjects: The Subject of the Experiment (called SE) and the Conductor of the Experiment (called CE). The SE is called upon to solve only a given task set for him by the CE, and if required, he must describe it as well as he can retrospectively *immediately after the experiment.* Of course, the CE knows the purpose for which he conducts the experiments, but he keeps his purposes secret, so that the SE may be able to describe whatever experiences he has in a perfectly disinterested and unbiased manner. Thus, a scientific experiment obtains for the investigator not only one, but any number of descriptions of similar experiences, and not only of one SE, but of any number of SE's. Furthermore, it enables the experimenter to observe the experience to be investigated under the most varied conditions. Since Ach, this process has been called "systematic experimental introspection."

Confusion of "Simple Elements" in Psychology. The second important advance made meanwhile by experimental psychology, consisted in recognizing the fact that there are two simple elements in the psychological process: one element in its very nature, simple or primary; and another simple by habit or, in other words, simplified and mechanical. Accordingly, the principle of method borrowed from physics, namely, to select the simplest possible processes for experimental purposes, could not invariably be applied to all simple psychological phenomena. This principle was entirely sound for the primary processes, but was unsuited for the study of the simplified and mechanized mental processes, which are not known in physics in the same measure that they are in psychology. As there is a tendency in our mental life (*Seelenleben*) to turn over as much as possible of it to a physiological mechanism, instead of using conscious processes, it was but natural that an entirely false conception of the voluntary action resulted. In fact, the conception of the voluntary action appeared to be weak and vacuous. In reality, when adults declare themselves ready to release a key upon a given signal, the act of will lies not in the execution of the task, but in its acceptance. The execution of such a mechanical action, on the other hand, can take place either wholly automatically, or it may obscure the act of will to such an extent that only thoroughly trained observers are able to discover it with certainty.

Ach's Experiments Include an Active Element. But, when this twofold advance in the method of experimental psychological research had been achieved, it became possible to investigate the experience of volition more accurately. Narcissus Ach was the first to attain great success in this very difficult field. He, too, began with simple key reactions, after which he caused more difficult tasks to be performed such as multiplying numbers, rhyming words, and transposing letters. In these experiments, the experience of volition was not in the foreground to any great extent. Nevertheless, Ach observed, as others had before him, that the entire mental process was strictly controlled by the task assumed. In most cases, it acts according to the character of the task, even if the SE does not think of the task. This remarkable fact was sufficient cause for Ach to discredit the theory of the dominant idea of an end (*Zielvorstellung*). But we shall discuss this later. Then, Ach proceeded in his experiments to hinder the execution of a resolution by interposing obstacles. The experience of volition soon revealed itself distinctly to the SE. If the execution of the resolution seriously determined upon was hindered by disturbing habits (a detailed report on this will be made later), the result was that the SE very energetically renewed his resolution. This gave an opportunity of observing a true process of volition at close quarters, and it was recognized that it is impossible to explain an experience of this in terms of images (*Vorstellungen*), feelings, and thoughts alone. An active element, an inner action originating with the subject, necessarily had to be included in the description in order to portray the facts.

Michotte's Experiments With Choices. The Belgian, Michotte, and his pupil, Prüm, investigated the process of volition, somewhat independently of the investigations of Ach. Unlike Ach, they took for the object of investigation, not a resolution, but a choice. Truly, if anything deserves the name of an act of will, it must be the experience of choice. The problem was how to call forth this experience by means of experiments, and to describe it as carefully as possible with the help of systematic experimental introspection. In the course of this experiment it had to be determined whether this process contained an element which could not be reduced to mere sensation, image, thinking, or feeling, or whether the act of will is merely an experience composed of sensations of tension (*Spannungsempfindungen*), gentle movements, and the like. The investigators decided to have the SE's choose between two arithmetical operations. Accordingly, they showed to the SE's on the experimental apparatus two numbers in every experiment. If the numbers were of four digits, the SE had to decide whether he wished to add or subtract the numbers; if the numbers were smaller, he had to choose, on reasonable grounds, between multiplication and division. As soon as he reached a decision, he pressed a key whereby the time necessary for the decision was registered simultaneously, and then he described the experience of choice on the basis of retrospective introspection. Naturally, two objections arise at once against this arrangement of the experiment. Are we justified in calling a decision between two kinds of calculation a choice? And if we are, does there remain a serious resolution if, as described, the experiment is closed by pressing a key without the SE being required to perform the action chosen by him? The questions can be answered only by the actual test, which answers both affirmatively. The SE's regard the experiment to be as serious a choice as other decisions in everyday life. This agrees with the experiences that all seem to have when placed in the position of a SE: The isolated experiment in the laboratory becomes by itself and in itself part and parcel of our lives, lacking nothing whatsoever in seriousness and significance. The fact that the arithmetical operation was not carried out, does not change the experience of choice at all, as was testified by comparing experiments in which the calculation was actually performed. The observation of the experience of choice gained a great deal by this abridgment of the experiment. For, even though the subsequent calculation when carried out in practice changes nothing in the preceding result of choice, it does obscure some details of the fading experience and causes unnecessary fatigue to the SE. This well-thought-out method led to very valuable results, of course, only after numerous careful attempts.

In Michotte's investigations, it was not at all easy for the SE's to separate the volition proper in the process of choosing. But the SE's proved very readily that at times there was no choice between the two kinds of calculation but merely a decision that one of them was the easier. However, these were exceptions. As a rule, at least an *external* decision, as we might put it, took place when the SE's, while pressing the key, inwardly uttered "add." These purely external decisions, being involuntary, differed very distinctly from those voluntary in character. In the case of these external decisions of the SE, they came as it were, mechanically, or they ran their course perfectly automatically.

Michotte Finds an Irreducible Inner Activity. However, it could not easily be determined for the rest of the group what really constituted the essential element of the experience. At first, it seemed to be a sensation of activity. The SE's are warm, they breathe more deeply, their muscles contract and relax. But, after frequent experiences of this nature, it was found that this so-called sensation of activity occurred also in the case of involuntary decisions; it was due mostly, as was recognized later, to a rather greater difficulty or to the lack of proper adjustment. Finally, the SE's noticed that the experiences in which they always had the feeling of responsibility were distinguished from the others by a real activity of the ego, an inner point of view of the *self,* which cannot be described at all, unless the ego be made the subject of the statement.

This inner position of the ego appeared in two forms: either as an assent, when one of the two arithmetical operations was proposed to the SE's consciousness, as if by another person or as a spontaneous decision in which the subject himself resolved upon one of the two possibilities. Thus here, as with Ach, the inmost kernel of the experience of volition revealed itself as a further irreducible inner activity, which is different from all other psychic processes, such as feeling, thinking, muscle sensations, etc. The general conviction of mankind of the existence and peculiarity of volition was thus confirmed by the experiment on this point.

Experimental Research Reinforces Common Sense. Only an extremely narrow mind would declare such laborious research superfluous, because the results of the experiments coincide with common sense and raise common sense to the level of a perfectly sufficient source of psychological analysis. Let him, who is so minded, remember that "common sense" was greatly embarrassed when facing the experimental findings which seemed to disprove the existence of volition, and that "common sense" was unable to furnish any information to the psychologist whose confidence in the prescientific form of introspection was shaken by many self-deceptions unveiled by the experiments. On the basis of Ach's and Michotte's investigations, however, we may ask any skeptic to repeat these experiments with unprejudiced SE's and evaluate their results. Mere philosophical speculation can have no weight whatsoever, in view of facts produced in this manner.

The Act of Will Has Various Forms of Expression. But, aside from this confirmation of the old doctrine of volition, experimental research has given us some further details which permit of a much deeper insight into the processes of volition than has hitherto been possible. In passing, an important observation should be made: whereas, in Ach's experiments, volition invariably appeared almost isolated because of the obstacles put in the way of the will, and assumed in consciousness such forms as, "I will rhyme," "I will not be misled," etc., this consciousness of "I will," as such, was obscured in the processes of choosing, and the SE was conscious only of himself as a person rendering a decision. Thus, inmost volition need not express itself in the words, "I will"; it may assume the most varied forms of experience. To a certain extent, it permeates like an animating principle, as it were, our inner speech — in this case the word, "add"; or as an external indication by a glance, or a movement of the head, or as an inner act of opining, etc. The same inward or outward behavior which is involuntary under different conditions, thus becomes voluntary and changes into ways of expressing the act of will. A most significant assertion.

THE WILL AND MOVEMENTS OF THE BODY

The Will as Horseman. How does the will move the body? Prescientific thinking (i.e., mere introspection) holds that nothing is simpler than this. The soul is found in the whole body and in all its parts, and therefore the soul that wills can seize any part of the body and move it as it desires. Just as the horseman directs his horse, causing it to trot, to pace, or turn to the right or left, so the will rules the limbs of our body. In fact, just as there are good and poor horses, clever and awkward riders, so there are nimble and stiff limbs, trained and untrained wills. Everyday observation seems to justify this simple conception.

1. *Patient Who Cannot Move Arm Without Looking at It.* And yet, let us see: here is a patient who has a perfectly healthy arm; he can make it move as he wishes, but only so long as he looks at it. If he looks aside, he drops the key which has been placed in his hand, and his arm is of no use to him. And yet, his arm is not dead; the soul has not left it; nor does he lack the will. Hence, things do not seem to be quite so simple; the soul that wills cannot forthwith make use of the limbs of the body.

Wiggle Your Ears. One might answer that this case is pathological; no conclusions should be drawn for normal life from exceptional cases. Well, at any rate, this case proves that a healthy arm and a soul that wills are not sufficient to bring about a movement of the body. Let us take an instance from normal life. Can you wiggle your ears? No? But you have all the necessary muscles and nerves. You also know what it means to wiggle one's ears. Please will it with all your energy. You do not succeed? Perhaps you should will it a little more firmly. Not yet? With your utmost energy! In vain. You doubt that you have the requisite mechanism. If that were so, you could not acquire the ability to wiggle your ears at all. But the movement of the ears is possible, and thus your failure is not due to a lack of muscles and nerves. This much is certain: the best will and the best bodily organs are not sufficient alone to perform the most simple movements. The will is not that most skillful horseman who does with his horse as he wishes, who grows with it, one might almost think, into one and the same creature, so that the horse all but anticipates the horseman's wishes and carries them out before the rider becomes conscious of them.

2. *Movements Accompanying Images Unconsciously Are Against the Will.* Now let us examine other facts. It has been proved in the laboratory by means of sensitive instruments that we can scarcely have in our minds a vivid image without soon performing slight movements with our hands or with the skin of our foreheads, etc., corresponding with this image. Mind readers sometimes use this fact with amazing success; they "read" from the entirely unconscious movements of our hands or the skin of our foreheads what we happen to be thinking of at the time. Again, I sit at my typewriter and keep on writing briskly. All of a sudden, my glance is fixed on one of the keys. Why? I do not know; it happens to be one that does not work. But it forces itself upon my attention as if it were the only important part of the whole keyboard. And indeed, before I notice it, I press it down as if from com-

pulsion, but with the perfect consciousness of making a mistake. It is said that a skilled piano player can play a melody which is thoroughly familiar to him, while his mind is busy with something entirely different. I can testify to the assertion that one can recite, word for word, a rather long memorized text while intensely occupied with other things, even with serious matters. We experience the same thing when climbing stairs; we move our limbs without always expressly willing to move them. Sometimes our actions are performed even against our will. I wish to stretch out my hand for a knife in order to cut the pages of a book, and I see at once that I have a pencil between my fingers, and do not know just what to do with it. Some years ago, I walked with a somewhat nervous, spirited gentleman through the streets of a small town. He was telling me about contemplated improvements in the town. "Next year," he continued, "we shall get electric bottle beer. Pardon me, I meant to say an electric railway." We had just passed under a low-hanging sign extending into the street, on which the words "Bottle Beer" glittered in large letters. Thus, the words had escaped from the speaker wholly against his will. To see the sign, and to pronounce the words were to him one and the same thing.

Ideas Discharging Immediately Into Movement. Psychologists have inferred from facts such as these that an image or idea, at least under certain conditions, can immediately discharge into the movement which belongs to it. In addition, a great many pathological cases have been observed involving disturbances of speech, writing, and reading. A person suffering from aphasia can pronounce a written word only in case he writes it at the same time or makes at least the writing gestures with his finger; another is incapable of writing spontaneously but is capable of copying; a third can write letters but cannot read them himself; a fourth knows how to spell a word and point out the letters correctly in a printed text but is incapable of writing the word, although the movability of his hand is perfectly undisturbed. These phenomena and numerous others have led to the following theory.

The Theory of a Necessary Preceding Image of Movement. There is no movement without a preceding image of the movement. If, however, such an image of the movement has been formed, the movement will follow of itself, if no inhibition appears, because the nervous excitement radiates from the center of sensation, which is active in the formation of the image of the movement, to the motor center in the brain by which the muscle is moved. Thus are explained the "electric bottle beer," the pressing of the wrong key, and many other phenomena. Images of movement can combine to form larger groups, and the combination can become very close, so that they follow one another mechanically. That is why we can recite a poem absent-mindedly, or climb stairs, etc. If the image of the movement is lacking, we cannot perform the movement either. Most people lack the image of wiggling their ears; therefore, they cannot move their ears in spite of serious effort. If they acquire this image by means of electric stimulation, they will learn how to wiggle their ears.

Then, images of movements exist in several forms. For example, optical images: we can imagine what the movement of the arm looks like, in a kinesthetic sense; we can imagine "how it works," how it feels inwardly when the arm is moved. If, therefore, the kinesthetic image is blocked by the effects of an illness, there remains the way of the optical image, which, however, is not very familiar to adults and, therefore, needs stimulation through perception as in the first-mentioned case of the patient who can use his arm only when he looks at it. Similar conditions obtain in the case of some of the before-mentioned disturbances in speaking, writing, and reading.

A Healthy Adult Without Experience. Thus, we come to a very remarkable conclusion which we can best illustrate by a hypothetical case. Suppose that before our very eyes a healthy adult is created, who understands everything we tell him. If we should call on him to touch his head, to turn his arm as we direct, to the right and then to the left, he would be unable to do so, unless the Creator also had given him the image of the movements. Neither could he walk, stand, sit, nor crawl, but he would fall to the ground helplessly like a baby. This hypothesis partly becomes reality whenever a partial apoplectic stroke stops the images of movements. Compared with such patients, our newly created man is better off; he still can learn all the movements. But how would that take place?

Exactly as in the case of a newborn child, such an adult would make a number of reflex movements. For example, the hand of the newborn child closes when its palm is touched. Furthermore, the adult would at random move his legs about as a result of some motor irritation in his brain. Now suppose this person, on account of these innate reflexes, came in contact with a pleasant object; thus he would seize an apple and that would give him pleasure. There is now in his consciousness a group of images, henceforth associated, whose parts we shall now enumerate one by one. The pleasure-giving apple, the goal, is in the foreground. To this is added the image of the seizing hand. At the same time, there is a consciousness of the "feel" of the arm, psychologically speaking, a definite complex of sensations – skin, muscle, and probably also of the joints. A definite stimulus in the brain corresponds to all these conscious experiences. In addition, a stimulation of the motor centers takes place unconsciously, by which the muscles are co-ordinately directed. According to a *general* law, these simultaneous stimulations combine and remain organized in the brain as dispositions or traces. If this record of traces in the brain is to be illustrated by a rough comparison, we might think of the production of a phonograph record: If a song is once sung into the receiving apparatus, it will remain engraved on the record, and the traces make possible the correct reproduction of the song. In a similar way, the experience of seizing the apple has been fixed.

If, later, the original idea of the end, the thrill of snatching an apple is revived, awakened perhaps by the sight of another apple, the nerve stimulus may radiate from this image over into the motor center and lead to the seizing movements of the hand.

Thus, the newly created adult should have to learn gradually from such experiences how he can move his body. To do this, he would not need as much time as a newborn child; still a considerable length of time would, after all, be required. As a matter of fact, this learning process repeats itself in every task requiring manual skill or in every free activity that we must acquire from the bottom up. However, we always have for such purposes whole groups of component movements with which we are already familiar and which, therefore, we need merely to insert into the total movement. But the more unaccustomed the individual component movements are, the more difficult is the process of learning.

Unconscious Imitations and Conscious Images of Movement. Two practical suggestions may be drawn from the relationship between the idea of a movement of the body and the external action itself. First, it is absurd to demand to oneself or of others an external action which has not been learned at least in its parts. For, the adult cannot spontaneously follow a mode of behavior which is really unknown to him, any more than a newborn child. It is quite necessary that unknown movements be learned. Of course, many bodily movements are learned to a certain extent by observation, while others are again adopted instinctively and quite unintentionally. A man of active mind who has lived abroad many years, and who is not unsympathetic toward the ways of the people among whom he lives, unconsciously acquires a foreign accent, pronunciation, and gestures. Without noticing it, he accepts the habits of his adopted country just as a child adopts those of his family. But, the school must not rely upon this natural but lengthy process of learning through unconscious imitation. The school must shorten the way by systematically instilling in the teacher and in the pupil the required images of movements. The truth of this statement is readily appreciated when applied to learning the movements of writing, etc. It scarcely occurs to us that things like manners, skill, courtesy, etc., are or imply an external mode of behavior, which the child cannot have acquired by himself but must have acquired either by unconscious imitation from its environment or have learned consciously. For the attainment of such desirable modes of behavior, purely negative criticism of a child is as worthless as the insistent admonition: "Be nice; be polite."

Attention Should Be Directed to End, Not Process in Learned Movements. A second practical suggestion applies rather to mere external movements. We have seen that the images of movements are impressed upon the mind of the learner simultaneously with the idea of the end to be attained. The more frequently the series of images is repeated, the more familiar they become, until finally, according to a well-known psychological law, a part of this chain of images drops out of the consciousness; i.e., is replaced by a physiological combination pure and simple. When this occurs, any attention to one or more of the links which have dropped out and are recalled to consciousness causes a disturbance. The series of stimulations emanating from the idea of the end in view would result in a much smoother and safer course if attention were paid only to the aim to be attained. Therefore, if a tennis player or a cyclist has once acquired the requisite movements, he need pay no more attention to them, but concentrate always on the end to be attained. The skilled tennis player turns all his attention on the spot to which the ball of his opponent is to be returned; the experienced cyclist does not watch the handle bars or the balance of his machine, but pays attention to the road he is traveling. This desertion of the consciousness from superfluous images, this liberation of the mind for more important considerations may, to a certain extent, be applied to the whole of life. Necessarily it can occur only when the requisite modes of behavior are known and familiar to us. For the phenomena of the movements of the body only, which we have so far discussed, are equally true of the movements of thoughts.

The Will Appears Superfluous in Bodily Actions. Thus, we have finally arrived at a conception of the bodily movements which makes the will appear as wholly superfluous. A group of correlated movements serving a definite purpose coincide more or less accidentally, and are especially fixed in consciousness by the greater attention generated by the successful action. Later they are revived, when the idea of the end in view — in the particular case, for example, by the sight of another apple — is revived, passes in proper sequence, and produces the correct movements of the muscles. Whether or not the first repetitions of such movements can arise only by and through the designated forces must here be left undecided. On the other hand, it is unquestionably true that many movements, which have grown familiar, are frequently called forth in the manner described without the medium of an act of will proper. From the instances cited, we cannot yet ascertain what role the will plays in controlling our external actions.

OUR PURPOSEFUL ACTION

Action as Merely Concurrence of Images. More than one psychologist has labored in the belief that the sum total of human activity can be explained simply as concurrences of images. In such groups of images there is, according to this conception, one image, that of the goal

(*Zielvorstellung*), which is particularly vivid, and therefore determines the course of the other images and movements. The intervention of the will is wholly superfluous, and, therefore, the will is to be entirely eliminated from the list of psychological concepts.

It Does Not Explain Purposeful Actions. If acumen were equivalent to correctness, the theory of the dominating force of the idea of the end, or superimage (*Obervorstellung*), would surely be correct. But, even the most ingenious theories must stand the test of reality. The theory of the mechanical determinism of the images under the direction of a superimage fits in excellently with our behavior while thoughtlessly playing familiar melodies, or "absent-mindedly" reciting long-accustomed oral prayers, and in similar cases in which the will does not participate, or even when the progress of the image series at times occurs against our will. This does not agree, however, with the occurrence of purposeful actions so familiar to all men.

Mechanical Behavior in Conscious Pursuit of an Aim. When we perform an unfamiliar act, when we execute a difficult manual task, when we carry on an important discussion, or when we seek to down an opponent in a contest, psychic reality presents an entirely different picture. Then we are in it heart and soul; then we mean to direct our every step carefully and with full responsibility; then we think we experience what everybody calls will. Now, as we have seen, experimental investigations have justified the verdict of common sense; there is an experience of volition. This experience then must stand in the foreground in the case of such pronounced actions of will.

It is accordingly just the experience of volition that we must add to the series of images and feelings in order to obtain the picture corresponding to the living reality.

It would be astonishing, indeed, if all our conscious life could be explained from the more or less accidental concurrence of group images. Our life, even our everyday life, would be devoid of real meaning. It is true, a single image may become dominant within certain limits, and may determine the course of other images, always especially vivid. But if we decide to stroll through a neighborhood with a network of streets, no matter how weak this idea of the end is, we shall carry it out with the greatest decision, in spite of the countless distractions of show windows, street scenes, conversations, and thoughts. Generally speaking, the most vivid image, or at least the most closely connected with as many other images as possible, has the greatest influence under purely mechanical conditions. Yet, this is not the case with those ideas of ends such as walks, which, though unimportant in themselves, are relatively hard to carry out. And yet, they are, as a rule, carried out to the very end. All mechanical laws would be contradicted if such an image, obscure, minor, and loosely connected, were to direct, lead, and duly complete such complex processes, bringing them to a satisfactory conclusion. We recognize how complex such a striving is in reality, especially in cases in which an indifferent aim is not attained. This happens either when, in the course of its execution, another more valuable aim appears to us, which we then substitute for the former by a decision proper. Or, it occurs when we forget our first aim for a few moments, and then turn, because of very pronounced habits, to take another well-accustomed road, until we ask ourselves in astonishment, "What in the name of sense am I doing here?" In such experiences, which indicate the conscious pursuit of an aim on the one hand and mechanical behavior, guided by extremely strong images on the other, there appears in our intelligent and purposeful activity another factor, namely, our intention – our faculty of will.

Volition in Purposeful Action. What else, indeed, could be expected, Experimental Psychology has scientifically confirmed the fact, of which every unprejudiced person is convinced with good reason, that there is a distinct experience of volition. Such being the case, it will be met with, in our mental life, outside the laboratory. Indeed, we find it unmistakably in the intentional, thoughtful actions which we perform day after day. It is a problem, however, what share this experience of volition has in the effecting of a purposeful action. We have seen that the answer to this question is not quite so obvious as it would appear. As has been pointed out, the will has no absolute rule over our muscular movements nor, we may add here, over our thoughts; many a movement, in itself appropriate, can now and then take place entirely without, nay, even against our will. How, then, does the will function?

ACH'S EXPLANATION: DETERMINING TENDENCIES

In the course of his experimental investigation, Narcissus Ach found that the act of will, as a rule, corresponded exactly with a resolution that had been made, even if the SE, for the time being, thought no longer of his resolution. If, for example, the SE accepted the task of multiplying two numbers flashed in the experimental apparatus, he performed the multiplication numerous times without remembering at the moment that the operation of calculation had been demanded as a task. Or, if he had resolved to form a rhyme for a senseless syllable shown to him, and the SE was occupied with totally different ideas and impressions, when now the syllable appeared on the apparatus, he, nevertheless, formed the required rhyme correctly. Of course, mistakes were made occasionally, but on the whole, the SE behaved according to the character of the task. Ach was justified in believing that these well-known, yet very remarkable, and until then unexplained facts could not be reduced to the functioning of a mechanism of imagination and association alone. Associations, which arise more or less accidentally and function mechanically, are blind to the nature of a task; but in the cases under discussion everything took place intelligently. He supposed, therefore, that a peculiar force, hitherto unknown to speculative psychology, which he called a "determining tendency," proceeded from the resolution to perform the task. This force was working subconsciously so that the correct manner of behavior might follow at the proper moment. In terms of physiology this would mean the following: the physiological dispositions of our brain are aroused by the acceptance of the task so that at the very moment, when the numbers or syllables appear on the apparatus, only the images corresponding to the task arise in consciousness. If the apparatus shows the numerals 5 and 7, the resolution previously formed, but now forgotten, will cause the SE to multiply them, so that now only the image of the product, 35, and not the sum nor the difference of the numbers will appear.

THE HYPOTHESIS OF DETERMINING TENDENCIES

Repeated as an Explanation. Still, very serious scientific consideration may be raised against the hypothesis of these determining tendencies,[1] whose functioning we cannot comprehend quite clearly in spite of all that has been said. We cannot present these objections here in detail; those who wish to study this subject more deeply are referred to the author's more comprehensive work. Only one point need be stressed here: the striking appearance of the image required at the moment is found also in experiences in which there can be no question of a resolution, and which can be explained by the well-known laws of association. Thus, this aspect of the phenomena does not demand the introduction of a new psychic force, a determining tendency. But, indeed, that was not the chief reason why Ach proposed the existence of determining tendencies. That seemed to him to lie in the uniformly intelligent conduct of mental happenings whenever a resolution preceded them; a fact unexplainable by the theory of purely mechanically functioning associations. The writer agrees with Ach that the intelligent conduct of our actions requires a special explanation. However, I do not believe that for this purpose we must presuppose a new force which acts subconsciously upon the physiological mechanism. An entirely new and unknown force is not easily comprehensible, and a simpler and more obvious explanation seems within reach. At the time when Ach introduced the notion of "determining tendencies," he still lacked the experimental basis for recognizing the act of elementary volition.

[1] Provided that more than a mere description of the phenomena is meant by this word. Cf. *Der Wille,* 3 ed., pp. 59 and 87.

Only in his second work, *On the Act of Will and Temperament* (1910), did he define the nature of the act of will. He could not, therefore, think of using the act of will itself for the purpose of explanation. Let us then attempt a simpler form of explanation.

Voluntary Attention and Will. It is generally known that voluntary attention exists, dependent upon the will. I am of the opinion that "voluntary" attention is not a primary psychic phenomenon, but merely a mode of behavior deliberately called forth because it seems relatively appropriate in recognizing a definite object. A detailed explanation of this opinion may be found elsewhere.[2] But be that as it may — attention and will are in any case very closely related — it is evident that you cannot will without giving the objective of your willing some attention. It has been found experimentally that voluntary attention can, to a certain extent, strengthen faint images. If two images of equal strength are within our consciousness, our attention may favor and enliven one of them. But as the voluntary attention either depends on will or is itself a will process, our volition can accordingly favor either one of two none-too-vivid images. *This faculty embodies everything that is needed for the explanation of the facts.* We do not introduce any new, abstruse force into psychic life, but depend upon facts which can at any time be proved experimentally.

The Cherry and the Grape. Let us assume that the appropriate movements arise to a certain extent by chance, as we had supposed in the case of the newborn child, and

[2] Lindworsky, *Experimentelle Psychologie,* 4 ed., Munich (1927), p. 220 ff.

let us choose as the simplest example two different movements which the newborn child is said to have learned. Suppose he has succeeded in seizing a cherry with his right hand and has repeated this movement several times. Some earlier experience has taught him to grasp with his left hand a grape lying at his left side. Now let us suppose that the cherry and the grape are placed near him in the usual position. With the two fruits in sight, two different but, let us assume, almost equally strong image complexes arise in his mind. He has the image of the seized cherry together with the optical and kinesthetic image of the movement, and he also has the image of the seized grape together with the image of associated optical and kinesthetic movement. The child begins longing for the red cherry; he strives for it, he desires it. Thereby, however, his attention is turned to the cherry and is diverted from the grape. Thus, he strengthens the whole image complex that belongs to the grasping of the cherry, at the same time weakening the other one. The nervous excitement now may pass over to the motor centers, and arouse such seizing movements as are necessary for seizing the cherry.

The Will as Switchman. Considered in this manner, the will plays, in a sense, the part of a switchman. A certain amount of psychophysical energy is present, and is distributed over the whole central organ. This continuously fluctuating energy is led to one single complex by a voluntary direction of the attention, and in our case to a complex connected with movement images. That is why muscular movements arise in this case. In other cases, when, for example, we view a picture, the movements do not appear because no images of movements are associated with this complex. Very often, of course, the nervous stimulation passes over into habitually associated speech movements. We faintly move our lips without being aware of this motion. If we discover the motion by chance, we do not suppress it directly by the inhibition of our will but by introducing another object of attention simultaneously with the inhibition. We shall return to this important point when discussing the control of thoughts.

Further Possibilities. On the basis of the foregoing explanation, we might do justice to the facts so far as they are known to us today. It is not impossible that future research will discover that the will is not only the conductor, but also the motorman who turns the controller and admits into the motor centers a particular current of energy which is present in the organism but which has been shut off until now. Still, we have as yet no safe knowledge of this and must be satisfied for the present with the theory that the energy, is directed by voluntary attention. For the practical training of will, this theory seems entirely adequate.

A More Complete Example. Let us now consider a voluntary action which is more complicated than the seizing of a cherry lying before us. Suppose the fruit is in a covered basket, and suppose we know that it is in the basket and know how to open the cover. We have in mind as the objective of our will not merely fruit as such, but specifically the cherry which is to be taken from the basket. Accordingly, our attention is voluntarily directed to this, and thereby the image of opening the basket is raised into consciousness. Now, the separate images of the movements necessary for opening the basket move into the center of consciousness, and exactly as in the first case the corresponding movements follow. The cover is opened. But lo, instead of one, I find two different fruits in the basket. If I reach to the right, I shall seize the fruit originally wished for — the cherry; if to the left, I shall seize a plum. According to the direction in which I reach out my hand, I shall, or shall not, attain the true aim of my original volition. What must happen? Of the two possible ends, my volition must turn to the cherry. Accordingly, my attention is directed to the right, and simultaneously the movement images necessary for reaching out to the right are revived, and I seize the cherry as I had originally intended. Thus, my will must again play the switchman, else it will not achieve its original aim. It seems unnecessary to point out how complicated most of our voluntary actions are, and that they necessitate choices at more crossroads than are presented in the present example. Therefore, whenever a crossroad opens, the will must act as switchman. Or, let us rather change the metaphor and consider the will as a motorcar driver.

The Will as Motorcar Driver. Thus, we have reviewed facts which are in harmony with our original contention concerning the existence of the will. And we have justified the common convictions of mankind as well as the teachings of the best philosophers who make our will the decisive factor in our lives. Our psychological theory has led us to ascribe to the will the role of a motorcar driver, but we have not yet decided whether or not he must again and again crank the human "motor," as our chauffeurs do, or whether this "car" has a self-starter. At any rate, the driver of the car is the one upon whom everything depends and who is responsible for the course of the car. Even if he sits apparently inactive in the car for quite a stretch of road, his expectant attention, which causes him to turn the steering wheel at the right moment, is his most important task, and in a certain sense the only one we expect of him. If he is absent-minded, the car will not necessarily stop at once; it does not necessarily run into the curb or take the wrong road; the driver may be handling the controls properly by force of habit. Nevertheless, the passenger does not feel safe with an absent-minded driver. This analogy indicates how we can explain the phenomena of purely automatic actions, nay, even such as take place contrary to our original intention. Generally speaking, all the facts which association psychology once advanced as a purely mechanical explanation of voluntary action fit into our theory without difficulty. As you know, we have assigned the mediation between will and muscle movements to the images of movements. Thus, we understand how a voluntary action fails to occur in spite of earnest volition, either because the images of the movements have not yet been acquired or we are prevented by pathological disturbances.

The Will as Field Marshal. In certain respects we have dethroned the will. It is no more the almighty tyrant carrying on whatever it wishes without limitations. The body is no longer an absolutely obedient tool, like the short-handled hammer wielded by the firm hand of Thor. According to this conception, the will, to use another metaphor, is rather to be compared to a modern field marshal. On the whole, the thinking for the field marshal is done by his general staff. The staff submits its plans and points out the advantages and dangers of each course of action, but it is the marshal who decides, who initiates one of the plans submitted, and who takes the responsibility for its execution. When this is done, the necessary detail orders are wired to the subordinate staffs, and from there to the troops. Finally, the spoken commands of the captains and lieutenants translate the orders into muscular activity of the private soldiers. The order of the field marshal has set into motion the whole widespread activity along the lines. The instant effectiveness of the marshal's order is dependent on many conditions over which he has no direct control. In fact, the more comprehensive and far-reaching the approval of the field marshal is, the more numerous are the conditions over which he has not direct control, such as equipment, methods of fighting, training of troops, and finally, the various liaisons of the troops. If one important liaison is defective, if only a main telephone wire breaks, the field marshal may be a helpless man. He can shout his orders as loudly and as energetically as possible; nothing will stir. But if every preparation is made to the last detail, and all is in readiness, calm decision alone is necessary; every pose is superfluous. The application of this metaphor to the "I will" is obvious.

CONCERNING THE POWER OF THE INTENTION

Intensity of Resolution and Energy of Action. It is a rather popular opinion that the more energetically we form a resolution the more energetically we carry it out. This supposition was adopted, as we have pointed out, by Narcissus Ach, who held that a force acting subconsciously proceeds from a resolution. If a resolution leaves in its wake such a determining tendency, it seems more than likely that a more effective tendency proceeds from a more intensive resolution.

Ach's Experiments Confirm Assumption. Starting from this thoroughly plausible conception, Ach conceived the bold idea of measuring the power of will as it appeared in the resolution. If we succeed in setting up a measurable inner psychical resistance against the execution of a resolution, the determining tendency will overcome this resistance so long as it is stronger than the resistance. It will break down as soon as the resistance is greater than the determining tendency. The slightly greater resistance may pass for the measure of the power of will. This happy thought could be tested by very simple activities. For this purpose, Ach had the SE memorize various pairs of nonsense syllables, for example *lap-tuf, mes-kil,* etc. Thus, he brought about a reproductive tendency: whenever the syllable *lap,* or *mes* is pronounced, the SE is inclined to pronounce the corresponding syllable, i.e., *tuf* or *kil,* learned in connection with it. This inward tendency is stronger, the more frequently the two pairs of syllables have been repeated. Accordingly, the strength of this tendency is measurable by the number of repetitions. All that is lacking now is to find a resolution which has resistance to his tendency. This is not a difficult task. If the SE resolves to form a rhyme for the syllable *lap* whenever he sees it, or to transpose the two consonants and to say *pal* instead of *lap,* this resolution will fight against the reproductive tendency which will have him pronounce *tuf* when *lap* appears. Indeed, the more often a SE had repeated the pairs of syllables, the more difficult it was for him to form a rhyme or to transpose the consonants according to the task. The simultaneously learned syllable always forced itself upon his lips. All by themselves, therefore, the SE's renewed their resolution of rhyming or of transposing the consonants, and endeavored seriously and energetically to make this resolution. But against a certain strength of the reproductive tendency which depended on the number of repetitions, even the most intense resolution seemed to be ineffective. The limit of will power appeared to have been reached.

Exceptions Which Require Explanation. Both the popular idea and Ach's assumption were thus confirmed by the outcome of these experiments. Only a few SE's could not succeed in reaching the limit of their will power. It is true that one of them committed what may be called erroneous reactions (*Fehlreaktionen*) in the beginning of the experiments, when the pair of syllables had not been as yet repeated frequently enough, and when the reproductive tendency was still weak. But after this had happened three times, he avoided all mistakes even after a maximum of repetitions of the pairs of syllables. Besides, he did not make an energetic but rather a very moderate resolution. At first, Ach thought he might omit this exception from his considerations. The SE, Oswald Külpe, the well-known psychologist, was familiar with the system of experiments and perhaps for that reason did not behave correctly. But on later repetitions of Ach's experiments, occasionally there were found SE's who also avoided the erroneous reactions, although they were without any knowledge of the purpose of the experiments. In fact, the Dutch psychiatrist, Boumann, who performed these experiments with normal and psychopathic persons, was astonished to find that the psychopathic persons committed fewer mistaken reactions than did the normal persons. Accordingly, there must have been an error in the whole conception.

Intensity of Resolution Not Determining. We said in a preceding chapter that we do not all agree that the theory of determining tendencies has been proved. We attempted to interpret the intelligent direction of our action in another way. According to our conception, the psychophysical organism carries the motive power within itself, very much as the locomotive carries its fuel, and the automobile its gasoline. The ingenious mechanical construction of a motorcar, with its rods and gears, had been provided previously by the associations formed in life, and carefully prepared groups of images were the indispensable presuppositions. Purposefulness, on the other hand, had been supplied by the willing, attentive, and striving mind, which uses the mental powers at its disposal just as the engineer or the motorcar driver uses his machine. Even if this metaphor is only approximately correct, there remains no more work for the intensity of the resolution. The switchman must handle the switch correctly, but it matters little if in so doing he displays great or little strength, so long as he turns the switch at the right time and in the right direction. In fact, if he applies too much force, he may injure the switch and possibly become confused himself in his work.

No Measurement of Will Power. Such generalizations, however, are of little value to an exact science. First of all, we must explain the results on which Ach's opinion was based. In Ach's experiment, the number of the SE's who, after a certain number of repetitions of the pairs of syllables, reacted wrongly in spite of the best intentions, was greater than the number who reacted correctly. Great importance must be attached to this fact and to Ach's interpretation of it. We have now compared all the experiments of Ach and his pupils, a procedure which is possible only because of Ach's scrupulously careful description of the experiments. Our restatement of Ach's findings shows that the SE's most probably entered upon the experiments in one of two modes of behavior. Each member of one group made a definite resolution during the initial stage of the experiment, before the memorized syllable appeared in the apparatus. Afterward, however, he gave all his attention to the apparatus. When the memorized syllable appeared, the SE, without noticing it, was placed in the earlier learning situation by this well-known and memorized syllable. The resolution of rhyming receded entirely into the background of consciousness, or even dropped out of it altogether. Therefore, the process of imagination was guided only by the associative mechanism, and the SE, contrary to his resolution, answered the jointly learned syllable instead of rhyming. The SE belonging to the second group also makes his resolution in the initial period of the experiment, keeps it, however faintly, in his consciousness, and does not lose it in perceiving the process of the apparatus. When the memorized syllable appears, it is possible that the jointly learned syllable also becomes conscious to this SE. But this is unimportant. The SE now refaces a double aim, the action according to his resolution, and the pronunciation according to his habit, i.e., his reproductive tendency. The driver is awake, and decides according to the resolution which he has made. If this conception, which we have gained from the records of the experiment of Ach and of his pupils, is correct, it will not be necessary to consider the mistaken reactions as a defeat of the strength of the resolution by the reproductive tendency, and it will be impossible to speak of the measurements of will power.

If Resolution Remains in Consciousness, It Can Be Carried Out. On the other hand, the mistaken reaction is readily explained when it is said that a reproductive tendency which opposes the execution of a resolution, no matter how strong it is, can always be made harmless if the resolution remains conscious. Therefore, it does not matter at all whether the resolution has been made energetically or moderately; so long as the SE was serious and retained it in his consciousness, it can always be carried out.

Ach's Experiment Under New Conditions. This result of immanent[3] criticism is in perfect harmony with all the facts reported by Ach and his pupils. None of Ach's experiments need to be regarded as an exceptional case. It is also perfectly in accord with the theoretical ideas on the effectiveness of volition which we had gained from entirely different facts. But even the finest theories remain unsatisfactory so long as they are not tested in terms of reality. Therefore, the writer had Ach's experiments repeated from the following viewpoint: in one series of experiments care was taken to have the resolution made as energetically as possible, but nothing was done that would cause it to persist in consciousness during the appearance of the stimulating syllable. In the other series, the resolution was taken without any emphasis, and was, in the course of the experiments, renewed merely by a reminder; but, the SE

[3] "Immanent" is the exact word used in the original. Perhaps it can be rendered more popularly here by the word "internal."

was told not to drop it from his consciousness. If the execution of the resolution depended on the intensity of the resolution, the reaction task would have succeeded in the first case despite the diversion, and would have failed not infrequently in the second case; on the other hand, if it depended on the retention of the resolution, it would have failed in the first case in spite of an energetic resolution and would have succeeded in the second in spite of the strongest opposing reproductive tendencies.

Confirms Previous Interpretation. These expectations came true in two respects: the energy of a resolution does not without further ado warrant its execution, but the retention of the resolution in the consciousness during the main period of the experiment secures its execution in spite of the strongest reproductive obstacles. Contrary to our expectation, another phenomenon appeared: the immanent criticism of Ach's records suggested the idea that not thinking of the resolution during the main period of the experiments always produced an erroneous reaction. But the writer's experiments proved that this was not the case. There are SE's who, in spite of their distraction, do not pronounce the memorized syllable, but either solve the task correctly or make a mistake different from the one expected. These SE's are not exclusively the most gifted, but often such persons as are easily captivated by a new impression so that the reproductive tendencies cannot be effective at all. The SE's gain time by this captivation, and the task rises again into their consciousness. This would explain why, in the Dutch experiments, the psychopathic persons committed fewer erroneous reactions than the normal ones.

Not Intensity of Resolution, but Presence in Consciousness. Summarizing the facts known up to this point, it is safe to assert that it is of little or no importance for the execution of a resolution whether or not the resolution has been made very energetically and intensely. On the other hand, it is of the greatest importance that the resolution be in the consciousness at the very moment when it is to be carried out; if this is the case, its execution is certain, provided, of course, that it is still a genuine resolution and an actual decision.

THE STRENGTH OF WILL POWER

Carrying Out a Resolution. Will power may appear in two different spheres: first, in the merely external execution of a resolution after it has been made. The obstacles which, in that event, may obstruct the way of the will, are, aside from merely physical obstacles, only these inner diversions which are produced by the process of imagination or by the oscillations of attention. The preceding pages dealt with these hindrances and the ways to overcome them. We have seen that it is not the power of the resolution but the corresponding inner mode of behavior which overcomes these hindrances.

Making a First Resolution. Another achievement of the will is essentially different from the preceding one, and chronologically must precede it, that is, making the resolution. We generally believe that will power reveals itself in the very act of making a resolution whenever the resolution demands a sacrifice. According to general opinion, the man with a strong will differs from the man with a weak will by his ability to resolve on difficult tasks and bitter sufferings, whereas the man with a weak will resigns himself to discouragement or despair. The same strength of will reappears when carrying out a resolution, as soon as new obstacles obstruct its way. Then it is necessary to make a new resolution, which is essential to overcome a new obstacle. The present discussion will deal with the strength of will required when making the first resolution and its subsequent execution.

What Is Will Power? Undoubtedly will power is required in order to make a sacrifice, and we are right in calling a person who permanently overcomes difficulties a man of strong will. In so far as such an expression means only the general prerequisites of a successful volition, no objection can be made to this conception or form of expression. But if by will power we mean a definite quality of will, we are dealing with a thought of such decisive psychological and pedagogical significance that we must first fully comprehend its meaning.

Psychological Formulation of the Problem. We shall state the problem immediately with great precision in order to grasp it in all of its bearings, primarily as it would be formulated by a psychologist. The first question is: are serious resolutions formed with a greater intensity of the inmost act of the will proper, in such a way that this intensity means the promotion of the resolution? Second, does a lasting attitude toward intense acts arise from the repetition of such intense acts, or moreover, is the lasting increase of will power (*habitus*) formed after the manner of muscular strength which is increased by constant use? These psychological questions refer directly to the existence of intensity of volition, not merely to its external appearance but to its innermost substance. If there really is such an increase of the inmost volition, the fact is of biological significance. We have already seen that this biological significance cannot consist in securing the psychophysical execution of the resolution which is hindered rather than helped by a more energetic determination. The value of an increase of intensity in the act of willing could consist in helping us to make very difficult resolutions. We may, therefore, conclude that, if there is no increase in the intensity of volition, it is not possible to effect either a permanent suspension of the will, or an inner growth of will power.

The Practical Question. But it is useless to burden the present outline of the subject, which aims at practical conclusions, with theoretical discussions of debatable points. The purely theoretical problem is investigated elsewhere. For our present purpose, we may state the problem as follows: first, are the existence and the significance of an inmost will power so manifest that the educator, who seeks to call forth acts of will in his pupil, must regard them as of prime importance? Second, may a lasting adjustment or a lasting increase of strength of will power be produced in the student with such certainty that it will be of enduring value in the student's later life? In other words, shall the general strengthening of will in the above sense be a primary educational aim? or shall we, after all, believe those who expect to provide the effective (and general) training of the will from any exercise of volition in any field? Some pertinent points of view and facts follow.

The Inmost Act of Will and Its Expression. Appearances favor the widespread opinion that a more difficult resolution demands a stronger act of will. But is this observation correct beyond every reasonable doubt? Man usually disregards the inner struggles which precede a decision, and overlooks especially the mysterious turning point which causes him to agree to a course of action. On the other hand, certain actions of will are quite noticeable externally. For example, when we wish to overcome pain, we grind our teeth, clench our fists, contract our muscles, and thus offer the picture of a person who works with all his might. Since all this requires much action, there remains with us the impression of powerful, or intense, volition. And it cannot be gainsaid that such external intense volition exists. On the other hand, the whole appearance of our volition is at times more, at other times less intensive. But what about the inmost act of will which animates these movements and expressions? If our inner volition ran along separately with our expressions, observation would probably be easier, and greater significance would be attached to the general opinion on this question. But conditions here are not like those which we described when we ascertained the existence of the act of will. The act of will is common to all volitional activities, and can, therefore, be recognized after innumerable experiences the more easily, as it is an unchanging feature in all the heterogeneous experiences. But if we attempt to analyze an effort of will accompanied by expressive movements and muscle contractions, the problem is and remains a task beyond the ability of the untrained person. The truth of this statement is more apparent when we consider the findings of Michotte, who declares that the act of will is not necessarily experienced in a special form, such as "I will," or the like, but that it appears in the form of the most varied and otherwise involuntary experience, in one case as internal or external speech, and in another as muscular movement, as it were, animated and combined with these happenings to form an experience. Thus, when my intense volition manifests itself in energetic, curt language or in a violent gesture or in a convulsive clenching of the fists, who will decide what part of my actions is due to the intensity of the inner volitional act and what part to the contraction of the muscles? Certainly not the untrained layman who is fully occupied with the aims of his volition and not with the observation of his volitional experiences. At any rate, it cannot be said that the increase of intensity of inner volition is an obvious fact easily observed. If that were so, we should not have met difficulties of determining experimentally the true nature of volition as opposed to the sensist theories.

Ideals and a Strong Will. A second important thing is the fact that strength of will is replaceable at least in individual cases. The man who has, according to the popular conception, the weakest will, may, from the standpoint of will power, occasionally become a hero. There is here no consideration of pathological cases. Examples of such heroes of will power were the uncounted German people who, during and after the war, made superhuman efforts in food-purchasing trips. These were certainly not all persons with strong wills.

In Munich, it was not unusual to see fifteen-to-seventeen-year-old girls standing at daybreak, in wind and rain, in line before the Royal Theater. These girls certainly may be credited with very considerable achievements in waiting there from five, four, or even three o'clock in the morning, and, occasionally even from the previous evening, until the box office opened at nine in the morning. All they were after was an inexpensive ticket. And yet, they were not heroines of will power.

I remember a former pupil who was regarded by his teachers as a person of typically weak will – a really weak man. The boy had, however, an ideal, that of becoming a smart army officer.[4] Many a person who observed this weakly young man seriously doubted the sincerity of his ideal. And still, in spite of a very great obstacle which would have caused others to change their choice of profession, he reached his objective. During the war he performed heroic deeds which cannot be described here without identifying a living man. It would not be difficult to cite many historic cases of this kind which justify us in drawing the following conclusion: everybody who is capable of conceiving a high aim can become a hero, and can achieve deeds which are expected only of a strong will, even if he has not the general quality of will power.

Great Will Power and a "Weak Side." On the other hand, the supposed will power often breaks down when the "weak spot" of a man is touched. I know a man who was from head to toe the prototype of a man with a strong will, ready to make sacrifices, strict with himself, and courageous in enduring physical pain. Yet, this man always avoided the doctor when a very minor operation might appear to be necessary. In these cases, all his will power was of no use to him. Perhaps the reader may think that the man with a strong will excels especially in enduring

[4] A good illustration of a "compensation." – *Editor.*

pains; that he who fears pains has really no strong will. What are the facts? In a recent history of the Indian missions, we read: "Formerly, the Hindus preferred dying by thousands to being converted to Mohammedanism. Even today, a Hindu will die of starvation or of thirst rather than accept a piece of bread or a drink of water from a European or a man of a lower caste." Evidently the Hindu are a race of heroes, a people of strong will. But two lines farther, we read: "The Hindu is a man of weak will, one who does not easily make heroic sacrifices. . . ." Thus, the man with a weak will is also capable of enduring pain and martyrdom. On the other hand, the will power which appears in martyrdom breaks down when there is a question of overcoming sensuality.

Training Does Not Produce Strong Will Power. Is marked strength of will to be found, perhaps, in men who have trained their wills? Does a notable inner strengthening of will, or at least a lasting tendency toward strong-willed action, grow from repeated efforts of the will? If an affirmative answer can be given to these questions, have we not positive proof of the obvious existence of will power? The experience of the monasteries, particularly the austere cloistered orders, offer direct experimental evidence in answer to these questions. The old Scholastic philosophers, who were members of these orders, observed that, generally speaking, the repetition of energetic acts of will, no matter how long they continued, did not produce a strong will. They altered the broad theory of an acquired *habitus,* and substituted for the *habitus* of general will power, the idea of particular *habitus.* They observed that many of the great fasters were too fond of talking, and some of the most taciturn men were poor fasters. Is it probable that continued practice helps at least in one single point, and that the will power is acquired in the particular performance of a particular act for which one has trained himself?

Mastery of a Special Trait. Some years ago, an educator came to me for professional advice. All his knowledge of psychology, he complained, left him in the lurch. His pupil had to struggle with an ethical difficulty and was painfully defeated day after day. The boy lacked even a trace of will power. When World War I came, the young fellow resolved to control himself for the sake of the soldiers at the front. And he succeeded completely in spite of many struggles and serious daily temptations. This went on for five years. If in any case, surely here a habit would be formed. After the war ended, the old weakness returned on the slightest provocation. The daily lapses recurred, but in far worse form than before.

Motive Necessary for Will Power. All these facts are explained uniformly and simply by this idea: *wherever there is an aim, a value, a motive, will power is found at work.* Where there is a lasting and ever present motive, there is lasting will power. Nevertheless, there are persons who do everything energetically and act with a strong will even if they have no particular motive. The objection is obvious. A broad assertion like this is more easily made than proved in detail. Suppose we admit the truth of the statement. What kind of people are these? Invariably they are persons to whom their own volition has become one of the most important things in the world. Most of them are physically robust. They have been able to assert themselves successfully and to enforce their will; they have found some who flattered them and others who yielded to them. Thus, whatever they have resolved to do has become immensely important to them, and they can brook no delay nor obstacle. Their strong physique has enabled them to express themselves in vigorous external movements, which has given them a feeling of physical well-being. Other persons again are weak in body, but their wishes, because of their weak physique, became all-important to the anxious guardians of their early youth, and so each of their wishes grew to have a special value for them. Both types of individuals accomplish much during life, but it cannot be asserted that they are generally willing and glad to make sacrifices. Often their display of will power is little better than obstinacy.

After all that has been said, it is significant that an experienced observer of human nature like Von Dunin-Borkowski has come to the same conclusions on the basis of long contact with adolescents. His views based on philosophical grounds are presented in a brilliant essay, published in *Stimmen der Zeit* (Vol. 100, p. 401).

Intensity of Will and Difficult Resolutions. Experimental investigations of resolutions to do something unpleasant, as reported elsewhere,[5] teach that we do not pass immediately to an intense increase of "I will" in order to make a difficult resolution. We rather try to emphasize in our thoughts, as much as possible, the advantageous element contained in every sacrifice and to minimize the unpleasant element. But if the SE is led to force himself to a resolution demanding an expenditure of energy, he will find

[5] *Der Wille*, 3 ed., p. 114.

such an experiment meaningless, serving at best, to temporarily stun the one that wills, by the feelings of tension derived from convulsive movements, so that he thinks no longer of the unpleasant sides of the sacrifice. If the resolution can be carried out, at the moment when the stupefaction occurred, by a quick word or by pressing the key, the expenditure of muscle energy may be useful. But if things are not so, the image of the unpleasant consequences of the resolution soon appear after the energetic "I will," and one faces impotently the bitter resolution until values are discovered in it, which counterbalance the sacrifice. My own experience has taught me how true these observations of my SE really were in life. Events in my life have since demonstrated the true nature of energetic volition. Such volition does not get us a step farther in difficult things, whereas the flash of a single value may at once induce us to willingly make a sacrifice. In small things, of course, the pose of a vigorous "I will," at the start, can produce the answer *yes,* which would not perhaps be spoken otherwise. However, such a resolution is not due to stronger volition, but to the fact that an auxiliary motive has been created by such a pose. We would be ashamed of ourselves if we withdrew after a gesture of this kind. But this is true only in small matters. If the undertaking becomes more difficult, most persons easily release themselves from the assenting *"yes"* which no one has heard.

The Doctrine of Values Accepted. It is gratifying to note that the popular conceptions of the actuality and significance of *strong, energetic* volition are giving way to more profound and psychological conceptions of the will. Thus, Mausbach (*Thomas von Aquin als Meister christ-*

licher Sittenlehre, 1925, p. 98 ff.) quotes the doctrine of St. Thomas to explain the intensity of volition: "As will itself is something that is good [i.e., is a value], the will may will to will." And thus continues Mausbach: "The energy and ardor of will . . . contains a willing of our own volition. . . . This intensity increases or diminishes according to the greater or less value which the acting person attaches to his own volition." No objection can be raised against will power explained in this manner. It naturally results also from the following doctrine of values: the more I appreciate a value, the more positive will be my attitude toward a special value which appears capable of constant growth.[6] Another noteworthy observation agrees with this: "These degrees of intensity of volition are not in the line of the energetic will, but consist in a plus or minus of what is seriously meant and of the exclusive nature of innermost turning toward, and devotion to values." (P. B. Barth, O.S.B., in *Benediktin. Monatsschrift,* 1925, p. 72.)

Repeated Activity Does Not Increase Power. There remains only one more mooted point to discuss: "It is a question if and how it is possible to provide the will with lasting power, a *habitus,* acquired by means of constant and uniform activity." Mausbach answers this question affirmatively and adds distinctly noteworthy reasons for his opinion. We must presuppose aftereffects of former actions as present in the intellect. "If they are present in the intellect and are indispensable for thought and action, why should they be absent in the will?" Contemporary

[6] It will be possible only in this manner to perfect fundamental volition; an outline to will one's own volition could easily be misunderstood.

experimental psychology does not, however, accept direct aftereffects in the intellect. It offers most weighty reasons, gained from experimental analysis, for the following propositions: *no elementary function gains any noteworthy increase of its power by repeated activity.* Even memory, as the power of retention and reproduction, does not improve by practice (of course, leaving out of consideration better methods of fixing things in the mind); it merely acquires a larger stock of facts to recall. Similarly, the capacity of thinking increases only in so far as the memory places at the disposal of the thinker a richer content of materials and better methods of thinking.[7] We must, therefore, revise the question quoted to read: if reason is entirely dependent upon memory for its progress, why should the will experience an inner transformation?

The Law of Habit and Value, and Will. To this Mausbach replies, "Because we need such a transformation. In the twofold nature of man, the ever-recurrent choice between good and evil involves a powerful, tragic element, which would be unbearable and senseless if the decision for good did not react in a wholesome way upon the will, and did not gradually infuse into it greater firmness and an elastic and free inclination toward good. The image of the oscillating magnetic needle must surely not become the image of the moral freedom of the will." We must acknowledge the correctness of the fundamental idea of this argument. However, the only conclusion to be drawn from it is, that provision be made in one form or another

[7] Cf. the author's experimental investigations, *Vorzüge und Mängel bei der Lösung von Denkaufgaben, Zeitschrift für angewandte Psychologie,* v. 18, 1920.

for a decision in favor of the good to bear fruit, because this is certain to facilitate all later decisions for the good. But to accomplish this, there seems to be no need for an inner transformation of will. For every decision for the good deepens the experience of the value of the good and facilitates the ready functioning of this value. Every good deed enhances the attractive power of the good or, to consider the figure of the magnetic needle: even if a restlessly oscillating needle is not to be made the image of our ethical freedom, we could be satisfied if the magnetic needle were kept at rest by a directing magnet such as is known to the physicist. What is achieved here by the directing magnet is done in our volitional existence by our evaluation of the good standing ever ready to emerge.

Value-Characters and the Will. This is the very point that does not seem to Mausbach to correspond with experience. "Mere training of thinking, the representation of motive and value" does not explain the gratifying success of the exercise of the will, since "these thought motives often produce an aftereffect only indirectly and without a new appreciation of value. How often do we see that people are in matters religious, political, or economic so firmly imbued with certain maxims of the will, that they make every individual resolution without any reflection immediately from their practical way of thinking; that is, from their firmly established volitional attitude." We do not see that those people make their resolutions from their volitional attitude, but it is true that they need no reflection in order to make a resolution.

The writer and his associates in the Cologne Institute have just finished an extended series of experiments in the comprehension of words. In these experiments we have proved that a great many words, even if the SE devoted less than a second to reading and comprehending the work, have their value-character in advance and without any reflection. As a rule, however, it is not the word that is in the foreground, for by means of the word the thing denoted by the word is placed before the SE's; and it is the thing and not the word which appears to them on the basis of experience very often before any reflection takes place as a pleasant or unpleasant, as a lovable or a repulsive thing. There is the solution of the riddle. If now a definite stand is to be taken, we may do so without hesitation. There is no need of adjusting the will; the value, or the nonvalue (*Unwert*), immediately appears and points the way.

Practical life offers numerous examples: political parties, religious denominations, social classes, institutions, etc., all have distinct value-characters. Their values for us seem to be stamped upon them. There is no need of reflection, or of adjustment of the will; we instantaneously react toward them according to their value-character.

Train the Will Through Motives. Let us repeat: we shall leave out of consideration the theoretical controversy, whether or not the intensity of the act of will can be increased and remain permanently more intense. But if I am asked how the will is to be trained from the psychological, theoretical viewpoint, it is for me a matter of conscience to give the following answer: choose the way which is more difficult for the educator and build up the whole of education on the significance of the motives. This cannot be done without utilizing the exercise of will to a great extent. Thus the teacher will discharge his full duty toward his pupil, even if the doctrine of the inner will power should prove correct.

THE MOTIVE FORCES OF WILL

Diverse Explanation of Motive Forces of the Will. What sets the will in motion? The most contradictory answers can be given to this question. According to some, only feelings produce a movement of will; according to others, only rational considerations lead up to a resolution. Some hold that sense perception does it. The more concrete, tangible, imaginative an idea of the end is, the more certain activity of the will must result. A fourth group even tries to explain all influences upon the will exclusively through suggestions and hypnotism. Each group points to certain observations in support of its opinions. And yet, it is clear that none of these contradictory opinions can be conclusive, even though they all are correct to a slight extent. The experiments of Michotte have made possible a basic solution for most of these problems which are, indeed, the fundamental problems of education. On the basis of safe and unprejudiced observations, we may now obtain a firm conception which conforms to all known facts and eliminates all contradictory opinions.

Values Move the Will. The conviction which all mankind has always asserted is true: *our will can be moved by all that appears to it as of value.* That is the supreme point of vantage from which unity can be brought into the various observations. Whenever an object appears to me that promises an advantage or a growth toward it, a desire for this object arises in me, and the resolution is made to acquire it, unless some obstacle comes in the way. Neither feeling nor imagination nor reason has prior privileges. I am for the moment indifferent in what manner the value appears before my mind. In Michotte's experiments, the resolutions were made without any emotional experience and without a noticeable activity of the imagination. Similarly in everyday life, I resolve quite rationally to avoid an obstacle, whether a mud puddle or a lovely flower bed, a harmless man or an onrushing motor car. But that does not mean that reason, sensation, and imagination can communicate values to an equal extent. This proposition must be examined in detail.

Earliest Values From Sensations. How do we, generally speaking, arrive at the conception of value? From experience in our earliest youth, we learn that certain sense impressions make us happy. The sweet, the gentle, and the soft arouse pleasurable sensations in us. But these feelings do not separate themselves from the object perceived, but seem to us to be a part of it. For instance, sugar in itself seems to us to be good. A piece of sugar becomes of value to us. The experience of pleasure conditioned by sugar has made it so. Thus, sense feelings communicate to us the first idea of a value. Later we get acquainted with other joys, other ways of happiness, and we develop, henceforth, by abstraction the general idea of happiness, perfection, and value.

Higher Values Conceived by Reason on Fact Basis. Accordingly, the value which is experienced first, directly and concretely, is the sensation, or rather, the sense experience of pleasure. But this is not the highest value which we perceive. We conceive higher values only by means of reason based on the comprehension of facts. These may be accompanied by feelings, sense feelings as well as the so-called "higher" feeling, but these secondary feelings are not necessary at all for conceiving the higher value. The boy, who is presented with a pocket watch on his birthday, comprehends this value very well and makes it his own, even though real happiness over the desired gift is prevented by a toothache.

Feeling an Accretion to Value. We may grant this much to the theorists who place so much stress on feeling as the absolutely essential basis of any resolution of the will: a man who never in his life has experienced a feeling of pleasure will never arrive at the idea of value, and, therefore, never can arrive either at an instinctive, or conscious volition. But if an idea of a value has once been grasped, the feeling of pleasure need not become more real than any other concrete basis of ideas. Even this may be admitted: whenever the aim of the will, which is the value or the motive which makes us act, presents itself, not only conceptually as such, but is also colored by the element of pleasure (for instance, the thought of a delicious dish of food), the momentary feeling of pleasure itself must be interpreted as a value and thereby an accretion to the purely intellectual value.

Imagination and Resolution. The relationship between imagination and resolution now becomes obvious. There is no direct objective relationship as was believed formerly, as if every image sought expression in a corresponding act, and that the more effectively, the more concrete the image. On the other hand, everything which is sensually significant has, as such, an intense emotional character. Most sense impressions are in themselves agreeable. That is why a colorful picture, made up of such impressions, has a distinct value. Moreover, such a picture may also afford definite pleasure. If, for example, bravery is presented to us in the guise of an attractive picture of a powerful lion, this concrete picture will have definite value of its own. In fact, the enjoyment of the picture may arouse pleasure in the idea of courage which it symbolizes.

Values Determine Choosing. Thus, values determine our choice. The intellect shows us the values. Sensation causes some of them, especially the lower ones, to be experienced immediately, whereas it may give merely a foretaste of the higher ones. Intuition (*Anschaulichkeit*) may serve both intellect and sensation in presenting the values. It is true that, even though thinking only can acquaint us with the highest values, it is feeling, nevertheless, which speedily releases our involuntary striving. I must first know the value which is conceptually comprehensible before my striving turns to it. I turn immediately to a happiness experienced in sensation before I can deliberately apprehend the object of value on which the happiness is based. This explains the power of emotional values developed in childhood, such as mother, country, etc., over other values, which are objectively perhaps higher, but have an exclusively intellectual basis.

NORMS OF THE FORMATION OF MOTIVES

Nature of Motives to Influence Will. Whatever is a value may act as a motive, whether this value is a feeling of pleasure directly experienced, as is produced in us by sensual stimulants, or is a higher value which can be grasped, only indirectly, by thinking. If, therefore, I wish to induce another's will or my own will to make a resolution, I must present such a value to it. But even if a value may set the will in motion, it does not follow that every value will make the requisite impression upon every will. The question, therefore, arises: what must be the nature of a motive that will influence the will?

Objectively Real Answer — Subjectively Experienced Values. The most obvious answer would be that a motive is the more effective the higher it stands in the series of values. That is the opinion of many parents, educators, and clergymen. Are there any higher values than God, eternity, perfection? Consequently, they advance these values again and again to their pupils and audiences, whenever they wish to move the will. But how often do these values have any effect; the average audience becomes indifferent and even weary of them. The educator and the preacher do not seem to realize that they must distinguish between objectively real and subjectively experienced values. Not every value that stands high in the scale of objective values can be immediately experienced by any given individual. The first hard work required of a teacher who wants to influence his pupil is to investigate the range of subjective values in the mind of his pupil. Subjective values differ greatly in a child, in an adolescent, in an adult, and in an old man. They are different for a boy, and for a girl. They differ for the child of a small wage earner, and for the child of a wealthy family. Within every social class they are different for every individual. Furthermore, the teacher must bear in mind that his demands upon the child are not the only ones which engage it. While the teacher tries to have the child prepare his lessons with diligence, the call of playmates and the attractions of play lure it out into the street. The motives I should like to stimulate, the child's will to diligent study, must present, objectively and subjectively, a greater value than the charms of idleness.

Influencing a Man Immediately. Two entirely different situations, which are not usually recognized as such, must be considered: do I desire to influence another's will to make a single, immediate resolution while I am present? or do I desire to influence another's will at a later time when I am no longer with him, to make a resolution or even an entire series of resolutions? If the resolution is to be made immediately, the choice of our motives need not be too fastidious, provided that they are morally unobjectionable. They are treated here only from the psychological viewpoint. It is enough if we succeed in presenting a value equal to the demand. It matters little to what extent feeling, imagination, or even moods induced by imagination, etc., are at work. The concrete presentation and the emotional appeal of a matter have, as we have seen, additional values. Feeling and imagination must be called upon to a considerable extent to bring about an immediate resolution, provided the individual to be influenced is responsive to the imaginative and emotional element.

Influencing for Later Action. The difficult task of influencing the will of a man at some future time, when he is no longer amenable to direct influence, is quite a different matter. This task seems to be considerably more difficult from the viewpoint of the theory of values. If the pupil's will would gain a definite direction and strength under the teacher's hands, the work of education would be much more simple and effective. But the educator has an extremely difficult task if he must contend with the possibility that the will adopts no permanent direction at all, but turns constantly toward the aims that appear valuable to it — as the magnetic needle turns toward iron. He must then, first, provide his pupil for life with values which are permanent in their very nature; secondly, he must take care that his pupil may have these values in mind when the teacher is no longer in a position to present them by his word and example to the pupil's mind. To find the basic principle involved in the solution of this dual problem will occupy us now.

Need for Permanent Life Motives. If a motive of the will is to be of permanent value, the object of this motive must first of all be permanent. I mean by object the alluring aim itself which is pointed out by the motive. If I move another's will by promising him a piece of chocolate, the piece of chocolate will be the object of the motive and the aim of the effort; it is not yet given by my promise, but it is pointed out by it. If I wish to equip the child with motives which are to move him after ten, twenty, and even more years to act ethically, I must provide his will with an aim for this later time. This aim which I set for him in school days must, however, be permanent, otherwise it cannot be striven for at a later time. Thus, it would be foolish to allure his will with the prospect of an aim that no longer exists, for instance, by saying in January to the child: "If you are promoted at Easter, you will be permitted to go sleigh riding." The object of a motive is not permanent nor lasting if it persists but ceases after some time to be a desirable goal for the growing child. I may win a child with tin soldiers, but not a man. Accordingly, the object of the motive must be of such a nature as to remain a valuable aim for every age. Such valuable aims are, however, as a rule, only the higher values; incidentally, they are of such a nature as not to be simple, intelligible, and familiar to the child. Most frequently they are values that, in a sense, develop with the child; i.e., they are so rich that they can be exhausted only with advancing years and increasing maturity. In our opinion, education must point to such values as early as possible. Incidentally, it should be added that the educator faces the added difficulty of finding a method of introducing these life values into the child's mind.

Thought Content Surest Guarantee of Permanence. We have just seen that the motive does not furnish the object of value, but merely points to it. The motive achieves this by all the available means; by communicating sensations, concrete pictures of the imagination, or objectives to be conceived only by the intellect. Let us call this the content of the motive. It is of no avail that the object of the motive is permanent if the content of the motive is not lasting. For we learn of the valuable object only by means of the content of the motive, and we can remember the object only on the basis of its content. Therefore, the question must be raised whether the three forms of the content — sensation, intuition, and thought — are equally permanent. Experimental psychology proves that feelings have the least, thoughts the surest permanence. If, therefore, the will of another person is to be influenced for later years, the motive must, first of all, be intellectually grounded.

Suppose I present the value of honesty to a group of children by means of a striking story. Let us say, I tell the life stories of Frederick who has become wealthy through his honest dealings, and of Charles who ended his dishonest career in prison. I may tell this story ever so graphically and make the incidents stand out in such brilliant relief that my young listeners are moved to tears. I cannot, however, depend upon its effectiveness in future years unless the central idea has been so worked out that it is fully grasped and fixed in the minds of the children. It would be possible to cite here many pedagogical devices which fail because "the dogma of intuition above all" falls short of anchoring the central idea in children's minds.

Motive as Part of a Train of Thought. In addition to the content and object of a motive, it is necessary to consider its structure. The permanence of a motive is not secured sufficiently by merely providing thoughts which are least likely to be forgotten. Research in memory has shown that the isolated unit of thought is far less permanent than the unit of thought which is part of an extensive thought complex. Complexes are forms of memory content, which are most persistent. I must, therefore, not permit a motive to remain unsupported in the mind, but must try to weave it into an extended train of thought. The ideal of forming motives would be reached if all the motives which are presented to the child could be united into a single, definite system. Thereby, it would be possible to guarantee the permanence of the motives, and a second task, that of having the motive in readiness to function when needed, would be achieved.

Motive Must Be Present. The most compelling motive

is of no avail, unless it is present in the mind at the right moment. Generally speaking, we take too little cognizance of the fact that memory plays a large part in our ethical conduct as well as in our mental life. The uninitiated is likely to suppose that whatever has been absorbed by the mind will cause an individual to react at all times in one and the same manner. That is not true. If no care is taken to cause a given motive to be recalled into consciousness when an opportunity arises to act in accordance with that motive, it is certain that half of the effort spent in instilling the motive will be lost.

The Motive-Idea Associated With Situation. The instructional methods employed in teaching the humanities, especially religion, have taken the necessity of the recall of the motive into account. As soon as the reason for a resolution has been made clear to an individual, he must also be made to understand upon what occasion the resolution is to be put into practice. In his imagination he thus connects the occasions that will arise in the future, with the associated resolutions, and as these occasions become real, he can recall the appropriate resolution. But this is only one third of the task. Besides the resolution and the corresponding mode of behavior, he must become conscious of the corresponding motive. The motive-idea must also be associated with the image of the occasion.

Individual Differences. One word more about the use of motives. The statement was made earlier that the motive must be adapted to the individual and that, therefore, the educator must concern himself with the values that appeal subjectively to his pupil. That does not mean, however, that motives can always be derived from values already established. Such a course would be in contradiction to the necessity for finding lasting motives. What is valuable to the 6-year-old child no longer appeals to the 15-year-old boy. One of the main tasks of the educator is to introduce new motives into the mind of the child. That is a rather difficult job. Primarily, it is necessary to reach the understanding and touch the heart of the child. The teacher can be certain that the child understands if he finds a connection with values already existing in the child's mind. Therefore, these values must first be discovered and studied. Some universal values, it is true, appeal to all children of a given age. And there are special values which are apparent only to people in certain social strata or professions, and there are still other values which are peculiar only to a given individual. It is readily possible to find common values which appeal to the average child, and to proceed from these in discovering and creating new values. If a child is slow to comprehend or is reticent or otherwise abnormal, the teacher will be obliged to observe the child and study its peculiarities until he can discover the values which appeal to it. Proceeding from the values discovered, he implants in the child's mind those new values which he can associate with those already existing. A group of excellent examples of associating new values with those most common to children is given in Forster's *Treatise on Children* (*Jugendlehre*).

Cases of Precocious Development. Certain individuals show such pronounced individuality in early childhood that it seems impossible to remodel their characters. These children are best understood by the discovery of the dominant value which seems to spring from their nature or early environment and which seems to govern them. These children are often very egoistic or ambitious or domineering in disposition. Inasmuch as these traits have developed in them into general values and it seems all but hopeless to supplant them, the process of "connecting with existing values" means something quite different from that employed with less pronounced characters. In the case of prematurely developed children, results are obtained by demonstrating concretely that the values to be acquired by them are fundamentally identical with the correct life values as these are understood. Such life values cannot be effectively presented nor proved; they can be suggested only as matters of personal experience and of conviction based on such experience. To illustrate: unselfish love of my neighbor must be pictured to the robust, forceful child in such a tactful manner that he considers it a forceful deed (*Gewalttat*). To do this effectively, care must be taken to avoid the direct statement that consideration of the rights or feelings of others is a form of forcefulness. Such a statement would arouse such a feeling of antagonism in the pupil toward all consideration for others that any argument would be ineffective. But if the child itself discovers from the argument the parallel values of considerate and forceful action, he will be placing at least some value on consideration for others.

Teaching New Values. In our discussion of permanent values, much emphasis has been placed upon the superiority of the intellectual element over sense perception and feeling. There is some danger that the reader may imply that the ill-reputed abstract or "intellectualistic" type of teaching is justified here and even recommended. A moment's consideration will reveal a vast difference in the problems under discussion. The first problem involves the retentiveness of memory; the second relates to the best ways of approaching the child mind and heart. In the solution of the first problem it is necessary that care be taken to impress the idea of the values upon the mind of the child because a complex of thoughts alone is certain of retention. No hint is here offered of the manner and means of introducing the ideas. On the other hand, the second problem "How do I teach a new value to a child?" involves other considerations. It is well known that a child is incapable of grasping an abstract manner of expression and a mere conceptual presentation of a matter. For that reason it cannot pay attention, without compulsion from without, and it tires easily. The combination of a lack of understanding, fatigue, painful effort, and the insistence of the teacher produces a feeling of dislike which converts a new value at once into what may be termed a nonvalue. Accordingly, any higher value must be introduced to a child in childlike language and concrete form and must be associated with personal values familiar to the child. Concreteness, however, must not, as suggested, choke the intellectual association of the values.

The Emotional Values Limited. Finally, is it desirable to employ emotional values in the first presentation of a new motive? Without question, the emotional values appropriate to a new aim must be carefully developed so that they are actually a new experience to the child. But it should be remembered that other emotions may be brought into play. The personality of the teacher may in itself be dear to the child. The presentation of the value may be made pleasurable in a number of ways: the eyes, the ears, and the other senses may find satisfactions which carry over into the value that is presented. But here limitations are rather close. A new value should not be accompanied with unpleasant sensations. The educator should assuredly seek a reasonably cheerful atmosphere for this task. But to set up essentially higher aims and satisfactions will likely be harmful. This procedure cannot be repeated often because the sensation is quickly dulled. Then the tones of sensation which are carried over soon disappear and the child suffers disappointment when the value is met in its everyday aspect. Such means may be used rarely and under extraordinary circumstances, provided an opportunity will occur sooner or later for becoming familiar with the value under ordinary conditions. A good example of educational discernment is to be found in the feasts and solemnities of the Church. The high points in the life of the individual – Baptism, First Holy Communion, Confirmation, Marriage, Holy Orders – are thrown into sharp relief by the rich but reasonable pageantry of the Church. This is true also of the Church holidays in which the community joins as a whole. But all these values are brought home to the individual by the Church only after thorough instruction, in the course of which the child has been thoroughly impressed with their essential goodness, so that in later life it recalls them in their inmost essence.

The Personality of the Teacher as an Obstacle. In this connection a word on the attractiveness of the teacher's personality is in order. The very fact that a teacher is disliked by his pupils is always a regrettable hindrance to the teaching of any motives which he may try to impress upon a child's heart. On the other hand, the fact that he is well liked by his pupils readily opens the way to the acceptance of any new motives which the teacher presents. But if the admiration of the pupil for the teacher develops into ardent affection, as it oftens does in adolescent girls, it becomes a serious obstacle to the educational process. Such an adoring child as a rule obeys request and carries out every wish of her beloved teacher. She is readily deceived into believing that she has understood a suggested motive when in fact she has not accepted it at all and does what is required of her for the sake of the object of her adoration. Such a case is not so serious; it is readily discovered when the same request is made by a person who is indifferent to the girl. More often, the child will deceive itself and the teacher, when the new motive has become valuable to it, not because of its genuine value, but only because of the emotional tones carried over by her admiration of the teacher. Sometimes the child will fulfill the request when it is made by another person, but the matter itself is likely to become quite unimportant when the affection has passed with the approach of maturer years. If the personality of the teacher has too fully occupied the thoughts of the child, it has prevented the child from adopting the objective values presented to it.[8] As adoration, at least in the life of girls, is an ever recurrent phenomenon, it must be treated from a biological point of view. As an abnormal phenomenon, more closely approaching a pathological than a normal state, it is not at all to be encouraged. The teacher who tests his teaching efficiency

[8] On the phenomenon of adoration cf. Ch. Büchler, "*The Mental Life of Adolescence*" (*Das Seelenleben der Jugendlichen*), 2 ed. (1923), p. 158 ff. 2.

by the display of affection which his students show will deceive himself rather completely. On the other hand, this natural phenomenon of adoration suggests how much girls need the guidance of a highly esteemed person. A gruff, repelling manner is just as inappropriate as a sentimental cultivating of affection. A closely objective demeanor, inspired by true love and care, one which in no way lessens the ethical demand upon the child in question, but, on the contrary, urgently insists that the ethical demands of other teachers and elders be punctually complied with in general, works out best.

MOTIVE AND FREEDOM

Is Freedom of Will Possible? If the significance of the motive is emphasized as much as it is in our conception of this subject, the question will be asked with increasing insistence: Is freedom of the will still possible? The older conception recognized the significance of the motive, even if it did not perhaps emphasize the motive so much in comparison with the inner powers which it ascribed to the will. And yet even the older conception did not find any obstacle to a free will, in the significance of the motive.

Experimental Psychology Offers No Single Fact Against Freedom. But let us first ask whether modern experimental psychology generally admits of a free will. I cannot name a single fact that denies the existence of real freedom of the will, so long as we do not mean complete irregularity or lack of reason for the resolution of the will, as do some determinists. We rather call the will free if, at least within certain limits of value, it can consciously strive or not strive for a value, or if in view of two equal, or at least not too dissimilar, values, it can deliberately choose the one or the other. Understood in this manner, the freedom of the will cannot be challenged on the grounds of experimentally investigated facts. So far as I see it at present, it is true that the freedom of the will is not proved by direct experimentation. Yet, I believe that the totality of the experimental results necessarily lead us to admit the true freedom of the will.

Metaphysical Objections Must Yield to Life. It is still less evident that the general human conviction as to the freedom of the will was questioned on metaphysical grounds, and just at the time when metaphysics was not highly esteemed. No one can assert that these metaphysical difficulties are particularly obvious. Even if they could not be solved in a satisfactory way, the objections would necessarily yield to the requirements of life with a *non liquet* until a more advanced philosophy provided satisfactory solutions. For human life is impossible without freedom of the will, because it cannot exist without genuine responsibility. But this idea must be explained at some length.

Human Responsibility a Fact. The idea of human responsibility cannot be eliminated from human life. Under certain circumstances, we invariably think that we are justified in reproaching others in this manner: you have done such and such a thing, when you could have done otherwise. All consciousness of being wronged, and by far the greater number of punishments have only one purpose, because they presuppose that the guilty person has done something that he might just as well have avoided. I was present at one time when an advocate of determinism very sharply rebuked a student because of an unsatisfactory report: "Pardon me, Professor, I was ill." "You had time enough before vacation; I accept no excuse!" was the answer. Thus, illness as a physical obstacle would have excused the candidate, if it had lasted continuously, from the assigning of the report to the time of delivery. This was not the case, because the candidate had been indisposed only during the previous few weeks. It was a question whether, during the weeks prior to the illness, there were moments in which the candidate could or could not have begun his work. If there were such moments, he must have been able to do something, as well as not; in other words, he was really free. If there was no such moment, the candidate was determined to act in a certain way either through external circumstances, such as sickness, and in that case, his professor should have willingly accepted his excuse, or he was determined to postpone the work by his entire inner disposition. That is just what the determinist says, and therefore thinks he is justified in uttering a reproach. But we ask: "Was this inner disposition produced by conditions which were in the candidate's power; i.e., has he ever done or failed to do something whereby that inner disposition was conditioned?" The determinist says: "Yes, all his past doings are to be blamed for it." We continue asking: "Could he just as well have omitted those acts at any time? If yes, he was at once free; if not, he is blamed unjustly." There is no way out of the dilemma. Either freedom must be recognized, or reproach is out of place; or again, it must be admitted that our reproach which would not be a free action, is completely senseless in itself.

Thus, let us suppose that the normal person is within

certain limits capable of consciously refraining from striving for an aim presented to him. We say "consciously" for, on account of the natural tendency of volition, every well-conceived value will bring an involuntary and instinctive striving in its wake. But this striving can be checked as soon as we are conscious of it.

I Am and "I Will." In the first place, it must be urged that there is no conscious or involuntary striving without a previously recognized value. The thesis "I can what I will" does not imply that I can really will whatever I am physically able to do. Physically, I have the means of jumping out of a second-story window. But actually, I cannot do so, unless I have an extraordinary motive for it. For my will has for its object only what is good for me; I cannot will for myself a harm which does not present itself to me from another angle as a corresponding valuable good. But if a fire threatens one with a painful death by burning, the escape from this suffering is a sufficient good to enable many a one to make the fatal leap.

Choosing Between Two Values. Our power of volition is not a possible susceptibility to an attraction, but a spontaneous choice, and is conditioned essentially only by the presence of a valuable aim. It is this fact that enables us to choose the lesser of two values provided these are not too dissimilar. In case of a great difference in values, the choice of the lesser means the sacrifice of the greater and the acceptance of a loss. In such a case, according to the universal law that we choose only what is good, we must have a special motive for denying a greater good.

Freedom Presupposed. Experience and reflection usually bring to mind a number of such motives. We have, for example, had the experience that the very act of not choosing a value may in itself constitute a value. In rejecting what appears to be a greater value, our self-will or freedom of action may be at work, and this activity has a value in itself. We may conclude, then, that the activity of our motives does not destroy our freedom of will; on the contrary, this freedom presupposes the effectiveness of our motives.

The Recall of Values. The question may now be raised, whether it depends on our freedom that the further motives, possibly the idea, "not choosing is also a value," rises into our consciousness. We answer: proximately and immediately, it does not depend on our free will whether or not to become conscious of a motive. Thinking of something, raising a formerly acquired motive into consciousness, is, primarily, dependent on recall processes which are not directly subordinated to our will. Thus it often happens that, especially in the case of instinctive striving, at least in the first moments, only attractive values are recalled to mind. But if only one good presents itself to us, we must naturally desire it. Our desire, therefore, is not free in this case. If we have carefully considered or even experienced the results of a given motive – if, for instance, a treat of some kind has disagreed with us – the memory of this rises into our consciousness simultaneously with the attracting stimulant. As a result, the essential condition for the functioning of free will, namely, the choice of two values, is fulfilled. The memory of a second value may be insured indirectly as well. For example, we may write down our first unpleasant experience and place it as a warning sign before our eyes. Or we can recall, or have recalled, the resolution which we made when we had a bad experience. Perhaps we may imitate the example of Darius, the Persian king, who ordered a slave to call out before him day after day: "Lord, remember the Athenians!" This device will be referred to later.

THE BASIC MEANING OF PRACTICE

Experience of Conversion. If the will finds an adequate motive, it is strong enough for any act. This explains why so many persons can choose a new direction for their whole lives because of a single important consideration, or because of a "change of taste," and then achieve with splendid will power, and without any special training, things that they never would have been able to do before. But this conception explains also the contrary of such "experiences of conversion," namely, the cases like Solomon's in which mentally sound people can commit in their old age, acts that seem to contradict their entire past. An apparent value need only assert itself in their consciousness, and the cedars of Lebanon fall. If we succeed in presenting an adequate motive to our own or another's will, training may be dispensed with. This fact has recently been proved experimentally in the case of school children: motives alone were taught to some, other children were drilled, besides, in the application of these motives. Progress in the desired direction was noticeable in the first group as well as in the second. But the value of exercise showed itself in another respect. As a matter of fact, exercise has a distinct place in our conception of the strengthening of the will.

The Value of Training. We shall try to explain the value of training in general, in so far as it is applicable to our point of view. In the experiments mentioned above, the educators found that it is far easier to explain to pupils the value of a mode of behavior if they are obliged to carry it into effect immediately; the teacher's argument for a value becomes more natural thereby. Apart from that, the following may be said in favor of exercises: the practical exercise of a mode of behavior desired by the teacher, overcomes, first of all, the imaginary obstacles. School tasks will serve as an example: school tasks appear to many a child terribly tedious and joyless, and even fatiguing. But after a child has tried for several days to begin his schoolwork promptly, he learns that the joylessness which he dreaded is not so bad. In addition, the objective values in the mode of behavior are actually experienced so that they no longer are believed to exist merely because of a statement of another person. The child learns, for instance, how pleasant it is to be free for a few hours, and to be able to play without the burden of an uncompleted duty, etc. If the training extends over a period of years, the practiced mode of behavior may become a real habit. But it must be assumed that there has not been coercion pure and simple. I would not lay too much stress here on the purely external *habitus* which necessitates an associative *habitus* due to the external movements. On the other hand, a definite mode of behavior can gradually become *my own;* that is, it becomes part of me. I am accustomed to keep my things in order; that is my way; it is part of me. And even if I have no other reason for orderliness just now, I am satisfied that I always did it that way. It has been pointed out repeatedly in experiments of the will that such external motives – found not in the matter itself;

for example, not in order as such, but in some circumstances which have nothing to do with order — were of amazing efficacy.

Training has, therefore, also a place in our conception. This is the more so, as the instructor cannot be certain that he will develop an adequately strong motive, by his word or by a favorable incident. And within certain limits, exercise seems to carry with it automatically a kind of external compulsion. Unless the child has been previously taken from its play by force and set to work, it will not, of its own accord, begin schoolwork immediately when the motive for such punctuality is simply presented to it. The teacher must, therefore, use his authority in requiring the child to begin its work immediately so long as it does not appreciate the value of punctuality. But the teacher must take care that the punctuality which he requires does not involve too much unpleasantness for the child so that the punctuality for this reason may become a nonvalue to the child. The initial compulsion must, therefore, be replaced by initiative which the child itself displays.

Average Motives and Practice. Finally, it should be noted that very long practice, continuing in some cases for years, is necessary to achieve permanent success in the form of a habitual adjustment or even incorporation into the ego. The experiments which were previously mentioned indicate this fact, and it holds good for all cases in which the educator must count on the use of average motives. In especially fortunate cases, life itself intervenes, creates unexpected motives, and effects in a day what might scarcely be attained in years.

Purely External Training of No Avail. Purely external

training must be rejected. This is particularly true if this training presumes that pupils can be led haphazardly to an act of self-control, and that they will thereby have gained some small quantity of will power for self-control in later life. For example, silence, if it is imposed merely by the ordinary supervision of the classroom, has no value as a means of self-control in later life. From our point of view, it may be asserted that training of this particular kind may be considered pedagogically valuable only if the pupil has been furnished with some motive for the exercise of the will. And only in so far as a special mode of behavior which is required of a pupil is based on motives which will outlast the school years and remain as motives of action in later life, only in so far may we expect that exterior training produces a gain for the later life of the pupil. The failures produced by many educational institutions prove this assertion. Whatever pupils are compelled externally to discharge their duties without understanding the reason for them and without having motives for their behavior, little remains of the good habits after they leave the institution. The phrase "boarding-school education" has become the equivalent of ineffective external drill which pupils discard as soon as possible.

II

THE PEDAGOGY OF WILL

AFTER having acquainted ourselves with the nature of volition, we need only apply our findings to the various problems of the training of the will in order to develop a pedagogy of will. In the first place, it is desirable to discuss the various proposals which have been made for the training of the will, and to test them in the light of the principles stated in Chapter I. In so doing, practical means, by which the pupil may acquire a motive, will be explained. The motive is indeed the only means of forming the will, and it is on this principle alone that we shall build up our pedagogy of the will.

EVALUATION OF SPECIFIC PROPOSALS FOR FORMING THE WILL

Hypnosis and suggestion, including autosuggestion, are not infrequently named among the means of influencing and forming the will. Let us speak first of suggestion. What is suggestion?

Suggestion. A physician comes to the bedside of an invalid – an inexperienced young soldier from the country – looks at him sharply, and tells him with some show of concern: "Your right arm is paralyzed." And, indeed, the patient whose arm is perfectly normal can no longer move the arm. Such processes are usually called suggestion. Two entirely different things are here confused. In the example given, the immobility of the arm is only the consequence of suggestion, and not suggestion itself. The suggestion consists in the fact that the physician imparts to the soldier a firm conviction which the latter receives uncritically and helplessly. But the act of convincing the man is not to be regarded as mysterious; it rests partly on rational factors, and partly on the intellectual helplessness of the person influenced. The patient naturally regards the doctor as an authority, therefore, accepts as correct what this authority, as such, tells him. He would not have believed his sergeant. The physician confirms his attitude even more by a firm attitude, by a confident tone, and by an anxious look. On the other hand, the patient is accustomed to regard the physician as an authority and to think no further of the latter's statements. Furthermore, he knows nothing of suggestion and does not suspect that the physician may occasionally experiment on a patient. So his conviction as to the stiffness of his arm is perfectly justified. The patient ventures no criticism because of the circumstances just recited, and probably also he is intellectually slow, and obvious counterarguments do not occur to him. An intellectually active person, who has some education and social standing cannot be treated so easily by suggestion, excepting in a matter which fear or hope easily may cause him to believe. A person with a hypochondriac tendency will easily succumb to the suggestion that symptoms of a certain serious illness have made their appearance. On the other hand, the idea of early appointment or election to a public office can never be presented convincingly nor suggestively to such a man; he will always meet it with a skeptical smile.

The phenomenon which results from suggestion is quite a different thing and does not concern the process of suggestion. It may, as in the case just referred to, disturb the imagery of movements, make the movement itself impossible, and assume the character of magic. But suggestion also may cause an entirely rational behavior. If I successfully suggest to someone that he suffers diabetes, he will quite reasonably observe the diet of the diabetic. The essence of suggestion is therefore this: conviction results not from understanding of a matter, but by reason of authority or an inadequate conclusion, drawn perhaps from a symptom to an ordinary cause. The conviction so established is accepted uncritically and is uncritically retained.

Autosuggestion. To what extent autosuggestion is possible may be understood from the above and from an explanation of suggestion. Autosuggestion cannot possibly be dependent on authority. I cannot believe a thing because I say it. On the other hand, a logically unconvincing conclusion may condition an autosuggestion. Someone has heard, for example, that diabetic patients suffer from thirst and that a healthy person, except in hot weather, should have no thirst. All of a sudden, on a winter day he finds that he is thirsty. Because he has a great fear of all sicknesses, he says to himself that he suffers from diabetes. What may be explained only as the result of several possible causes, appears to him as the result of only one cause because anxiety paralyzes further reasoning and does not allow a critical consideration of facts. Without his anxiety, this man would remember that he had herring for luncheon and that his thirst is quite normal.

Suggestion Is Morally Admissible. From what has been said, the significance and justification of suggestion in forming and influencing the will becomes clear. The conviction which is acquired so uncritically is not necessarily erroneous. Moreover, there may be circumstances when, on the one hand, it is absolutely necessary to impart quickly to another person a conviction and to insure the resultant behavior. This is true when the usual way of convincing him is not possible. If it is a question of saving oneself from a burning building, the idea of danger must be imparted at a moment's notice to those who are not yet immediately aware of it; any critical discussion may be fatal. That is why it is perfectly justifiable to choose means which preclude critical consideration, as for example, by an exclamation of fright and gestures of fleeing. In other words, in this case suggestion is necessary and morally admissible.

Second, many things involve suggestion of necessity, even if suggestion is not intended. He who is convinced that in prayer he stands before God, will and must express this by his whole attitude. But this attitude will have a suggestive effect on the observing child; i.e., it will take up the conviction of God's proximity in such a manner that critical considerations cannot arise in its mind. Then it will act according to this conviction. What is illustrated here by prayer, takes place naturally in countless other fields. The conduct of adults in patriotic, economic, hygienic, and similar important matters inoculates the child with convictions against which criticism cannot assail for years to come. If we take into account that a whole series of such convictions and such suggestions are forced upon the individual from his earliest childhood, we know that because of their great number it is impossible to digest them intellectually to any extent.

Need for Rational Foundations for These Convictions. People are often in error who call convictions, awakened in this manner in the child, instincts. Man has but very few instincts. Human nature does not need instincts as do animals, for the reason that, in man, they can be dispensed with partly because of the care exercised by the parents, partly because of the possibility of suggestion, and finally because of the capacity for learning. This suggestion, inevitably a part of human nature, is an educational means intended as such by nature, and has a harmful effect only in so far as some suggestions involuntarily create erroneous convictions. Viewed from this biological point of view, the suggestion of the example cannot be condemned so long as the example itself is not silly comedy, but is sincere. Nor will it be necessary to supplement the suggestion of example by teaching the growing child the critical points of view to add to an accepted conviction. It will rather be necessary gradually to furnish the rational foundations for the conviction which has been uncritically adopted, and thereby to prepare the child by degrees for critical thought during the years of adolescence. A goodly part of the inner storms and struggles of that time is surely to be traced back to the fact that many vitally important suggestions did not receive their motivation in time; they did not become the child's own convictions; they now cause a tangle of the strongest doubts that rage in the youthful mind.

Limit of Suggestion in Education. But here the limits

of suggestion in education are also indicated. Whenever the possibility of suggesting the basis for a vitally important conviction is offered, the foundation must be laid at the same time. It is true that a momentary guidance of will is possible and justified by a suggestion, but a permanent disposition results at best only in the case of intellectually dependent individuals. Certainly the means of education must not be judged in terms of inferior persons.

Couéism. Autosuggestion has less basis than suggestion to direct one's volition. This assertion is borne out quite completely by the failure of various systems of autosuggestion, like Couéism, which is still in vogue. The method of Coué, who was at one time a pharmacist, may be described in brief as follows: a person who wishes to enjoy some desirable physical or mental condition need only repeat to himself a prescribed formula twenty times each morning and evening. If, for example, a man wants to rid himself of a headache and possess a clear head, or overcome timidity and acquire a courageous spirit, he will simply repeat slowly and thoughtfully the formula "I will be clearheaded," or "I will be courageous." The same formula based on Coué's model is recommended by Kruse in his book, *I Will – I Can.* The formula need not be pronounced as a resolution; in fact, Coué argues that volition be eliminated as far as possible from the recital of the formula.[1] He builds on the theory, advocated in

[1] When speaking of the harmfulness and uselessness of volition, Coué sensed something of the truth; namely, that the supposedly energetic "I Will," which we also have rejected, is worthless. But on account of the insufficiency of his psychological conceptions he is mistaken when he believes that he can eliminate volition entirely, and he must abandon the entire guidance of the mind to imagination. Evidently, there is need eventually of will in order to follow Coué's advice at all.

France by Pierre Janet and now entirely repudiated, that every idea tends to realize itself in action. This theory leads Coué to believe that one must repeat to oneself an idea each morning and evening, in order that it may sink into the subconsciousness and from there be carried into realization. The facts on which the theory is based were enumerated on pages 48–50. In these cases, it is true that a movement immediately follows an image, but not because the image as such produces the movement – (no matter how ardently or energetically I think of a million dollars, I will not get them) – but because the images were formerly associated with a movement, as has been described. Coué's idea originated in a low level of research on the will, and is completely fallacious.

REASONS FOR COUÉ'S SUCCESS

And yet, Coué has achieved amazingly successful cures, so that now, after his death, a very profitable business is made of Couéism. What is the cause of this success? First of all, a man in blissful ignorance of the matter will believe in Coué's prescription, and will be animated by the happy hope that his suffering will be relieved. A cheerful state of the mind, however, is for physiological reasons the most favorable physical disposition in which the healing powers that are active in all organisms can operate successfully. The man who seriously believes in the healing power of a remedy will not stop to concern himself day by day about his condition. In simply forgetting his troubles he will avoid looking for the symptoms. Consequently, he will not aggravate them nor cause them to recur by association. Such physical conditions like blushing, rush of blood to the head, the release of glandular secretions are closely associated with thinking of them and recur by reason of thinking of them. The man will, therefore, no longer direct his attention to the diseased part of his body, and will obviate the unfavorable physiological effects which such one-sided concentration produces. The recital of the foregoing facts will immediately suggest the limitations as well as the conditions under which this method of treatment is effective. It depends in no way upon correct theory nor upon good technique in application, but upon mere faith in its effectiveness.

Coué's movement was a repetition of the success achieved by the Christian Science movement, which taught that one should stretch out comfortably on a couch in the firm conviction that the current of divine power would flow in a healing stream through one's body.

A certain degree of novelty is necessarily associated with such "cures." At the beginning the new movement invariably attracts enthusiastic followers. These are enabled to apply the method to persons who are psychically conditioned and, therefore, the cures are successful. Others are, in turn, filled with the confidence necessary for still further cures. However, as the movement spreads, criticism starts and spreads; the successful treatments become more rare as time passes; and finally the movement collapses. Couéism and its imitators who are certain to appear in the future will fare in the same way. Such autosuggestive cures find more difficult obstacles in true organic troubles. The fracture of a leg or a case of advanced appendicitis do not admit of an associative treatment. Unfortunately, the cheap and painless remedy of autosuggestion has been resorted to in many such cases and has been the cause of untimely deaths.

A Living Christianity. Cannot Couéism, Christian Science, and similar insufficiently motivated panaceas be replaced by something better? Surely far better means of curing human ills are offered in the Gospel where we may read how the "lilies of the field" and "the birds of the air" thrive, because God Himself cares for them. And does not the Saviour forbid us to worry but to leave all care to the heavenly Father without whose wise and loving providence not even a hair falls from our heads. One need only take Christianity seriously to be prepared to imitate St. Francis of Assisi, and to strip oneself of all possessions and lead a life of poverty and hardship without fear of physical consequences. Even though he may lack all worldly means, he will have courage for any undertaking which he may consider pleasing to the will of God. The classic reply of St. Theresa will be recalled, when charged with recklessness in opening her religious houses with insufficient funds: "Theresa and these few pence cannot support these houses; but these pence, and Theresa, and God will be sufficient." But where can we find such living Christianity?

Hypnotism. The essential procedure of hypnotism consists in the following: some conviction is imparted to the patient while in a cataleptic state. Critical judgment is at the same time excluded chiefly as the result of this somnolent condition of the patient. Furthermore, a complex combination of images, suited to the aims of the physician, is produced. If, for example, the patient has agoraphobia, and fears to cross an open field, it is suggested to him in the hypnotic state that at a certain hour he will wish to walk across the field. Or, it may be suggested that the patient whistle a certain ditty at the stroke of three. By this suggestion, an association is established between the image of the stroke of the clock and that of the song so that, at the stroke of the clock, the ditty-imagery arises with the associated movement images and brings about by itself the desire to whistle the song. Such artificial combinations of images, connected with an artificial exclusion of the ordinary process of imagery, naturally has less duration in the degree that the hypnotic influence fails to change the natural *habitus* of the patient. If such influences are to remain permanently and to act without fail, we must aim at getting the patient very gradually and easily into a hypnotic state. It happens eventually that a person who is frequently hypnotized relapses by himself into the state of hypnosis at the stroke of a clock, or in view of certain impressions, even if the hypnotist is not present in person. In this renewed hypnotic state, he acts according to the instructions which he formerly received from the hypnotist. But it is manifest that the use of such an abnormal state can never be an objective in a conscientious scheme of education.

Hypnosis Not an Educational Procedure. Hypnosis and similar processes are not ordinary means at the command of the educator. Hypnotism can be applied only to the cure of nervous disturbances or conditions which have developed on the basis of neurosis. It must be used only by an experienced physician, when in the judgment of a conscientious expert no other remedies are available. On the other hand, hypnosis can never permanently remove a passion. Even if it temporarily removes the stimuli originating in the organism; e.g., the stimulus to drinking, and even if for a short time it diverts the mind from the dangerous goal, it, nevertheless, is ineffective if it is not supported immediately by positive moral education. Finally, it cannot achieve the main task of education — the inculcation of high ideals and values. Accordingly, all means which approach the hypnotic procedure must be discarded in self-education as well as in the education of others.

RIGHT AND WRONG WAYS OF THOUGHT CONTROL

The Focus of Consciousness. In the educational process the greatest emphasis must be placed on the cultivation of motives. Motives for or against our volitional striving reach us at all times intellectually. For this reason, thought control is always very significant in the control of our own wills. If our will naturally strives for everything that presents itself as something good, it resembles the magnetic needle which turns now to the right, and then to the left, when an attracting piece of iron is held close to it. In that case there can be no question of firmness of character. If we admit the thought of a pseudo value into our minds only once, it will soon hold our attention and become the center of our consciousness, superseding all thought of other values. Even if we reject the Herbartian concept of the battle of images, we come very near the psychological facts when we speak of the battle between different values, which are contending for the focus of consciousness. We have shown that the mind tends to react without inhibition to the individual value that is singly before it.

Conflict of Values and Thought Control. But the pseudo values are better prepared than the true values to take up the struggle for supremacy. Even if we leave entirely out of consideration the religious and supernatural element, the higher values of life are to be gained only through more or less abstract recognition by the intellect and can be presented only by way of general concepts. Thus, the child can scarcely picture to itself concretely the value of a carefree and respectable station in life. It does not even understand easily that there is a higher value in a higher station. Consequently, he wishes to become a confectioner, a chauffeur, or the like. It is still more difficult to have the child understand that values are attached to the faithful and regular discharge of duty, a means to reach those higher callings. Similarly it is difficult to make a child appreciate the social values of truthfulness, fidelity, and so forth. These abstract values are overshadowed by the immediately concrete and clearly pleasant values. A piece of cake gives immediate and delightful sensual pleasure. The escape from the classroom into the street promises at once an easily imagined happiness. Thus, the easily imagined values which are associated with vivid sensations, fight against values which are reproduced with difficulty and are connected with moderate sensations. Therefore, the latter are from the start at a disadvantage, unless voluntary guidance of the thoughts interferes in their behalf. There seems to be no need of discussing the fact at length that this uneven fight gains a special significance as soon as sexual stimuli are aroused and powerful sensations of the organs are made to fight for the possession of consciousness. Therefore, the ability of thought control is of utmost importance, particularly in the moral life.

Control of Thoughts and of Body. How can we guide

our thoughts? The question has been answered in a fundamental way in the first chapter, for our thoughts are to be guided exactly as our bodily movements are. We have no greater control of the trend of our thought than of the process of muscular movements. Even there the will cannot interfere directly. I cannot, by the command of my will, destroy a thought and without further ado enthrone another thought.

The Will Directs Attention. Thoughts arise always on the basis of the reproductive mechanism, whose play is determined in the first place by the condition of the brain. So far as we know at present, the will can interfere there only by directing the attention at its discretion to one or another image, when several are afforded, and by turning the trend of thought into other channels.

Will Does Not Determine Mechanism of Imagery. The redirection of thought is possible and actually takes place only under certain conditions. It is impossible if there are not several images in consciousness at the same time. But the fact that one or several images appear in our minds is not determined in the first place by the will. The mechanism of imagery, or rather our external perception, is the first means of producing phantasms as they arise; we may simultaneously consider several percepts. If the several things are at the same time in consciousness, our will can at pleasure turn toward one of them, provided it actually has a motive necessary for making a decision.

The Way to Control Thoughts. Such motives are, however, like all thoughts, not present at the very beginning. They must be experienced gradually. Yet the mere fact that we have once learned them does not suffice; care must be taken further that they enter our consciousness at the right moment; that is, at the moment, when the agreeable thought or the thought which should be avoided, arises.

We have noted in the first section of this book that the will cannot achieve this directly, but only in a roundabout way. If I just learn the harmfulness of a new train of thought, I can establish a firm association between this thought and the harmfulness of the train of thoughts. Or, I can possibly set up for myself a warning in the form of a motto in the spot where the thought occurs to me. But these are feeble makeshifts. A far more effective device than a voluntary association of thoughts will be at my command if I firmly weld the undesired thought to an unpleasant experience, or if I weigh the bad consequences of the thought in such a way that the thought is, as it were, branded as evil. It cannot then arise in my mind without showing the "brand of infamy" (*Schandmal*) on its forehead.

It is indeed a very long way that leads to the sure control of the thoughts. First, the harmful thought must be known as such; then, an experience is necessary to show its destructiveness, and this experience must be associated with the harmful thought. In addition to this, the process must become conscious again, or must at least be applied in a practical sense. Of course, education can and must shorten this long way, which involves so many dangers. Brief reflection will reveal to the reader how this is feasible and why it is advisable.

Now, there will be no need for special inner strength for the guidance of thoughts, if it is necessary merely to direct the attention to one of several thoughts or to divert it from one of these thoughts. The individual will need merely the guidance of his will to direct his attention or, to repeat the figure which we used earlier in this book, he will merely need to "throw the switch." This leads us to a discussion of certain ineffective means of guiding thought.

The Effect of an Energetic "No!" As a rule, persons who are scrupulous from religious motives, and who for this reason are given to scrutinizing their thoughts, are easily led to utter an energetic "No!" or "Away!" when they perceive a dangerous thought. The utterance is naturally joined with the shaking of the head or a protesting gesture of the hand or even the stamping of the foot. A widely advertised method of will training actually recommends these actions, because in the opinion of the promoters the thread of our thoughts will be torn by a forceful "No!" Here again the disadvantage of popular language applied to scientific matters appears, and erroneous conclusions are drawn from the metaphor which describes our experience as a thread of thought. What are the psychological facts? He who utters the expression "No" because of scrupulosity, intends thereby to ethically rid himself of the thought and declare that he has no share in it, in order to be personally sure that he has not sinned by such a thought. It may be noted, incidentally, that this attitude is often very egotistic, especially when such a person deems the consciousness of his sinlessness more valuable than the unhesitating discharge of his duties, which often require that he shall not give way to such an intellectual standstill. He thinks apparently that he can drive away by his energetic "No!" every thought as if it were a living enemy.

The Psychological Effects. But what happens psychologically? Certainly, in the first moment only "No" stands in the foreground of consciousness and is momentarily a relief from the vexatious thought. But after a few seconds, the "No" fades away. On the other hand, the unpleasant thought, which had been driven somewhat into the background, comes into the foreground again because of the tendency of persistence. As the thought has strong reserves, namely, all the images and organic sensations that are associated with it, it is again the sole possessor of consciousness. The tormented person, however, calls again upon this "No," and after he experiences its impotence several times, he becomes discouraged. Indeed he has achieved only one thing, that of having associated the thought to be avoided with a number of new impressions, a fact which makes the thought even more powerful for the future. If, in addition, the tempted person has tired himself and exhausted his nerves in this struggle, he will be even more incapable of future resistance.

Why the "No" Is Ineffective. Why then is this "No" ineffective? First of all, because the supposition of the will's direct influence on the trend of thought is wrong. What has morally a certain justification as a renunciation remains psychologically ineffective. It weakens the troublesome thought for a short while, or drives the thought into the background. But as this "No" stands perfectly isolated in consciousness and offers no stimulant to the attention, the previous state of consciousness returns immediately. A thought, it must be remembered, can be driven away only by another thought or by another intellectual occupation. This other intellectual occupation must have a double character. First, it must outlast the tendency of persistence of the thought to be driven away. The tendency of persistence of an isolated image lasts indeed for just a few seconds only. But attractive thoughts (and the same holds good of disquieting ones) are not isolated but are associated with many others and accompanied by more enduring organic sensations, so that with the help of all these factors they can be brought back to consciousness for a considerable length of time. Furthermore, the diverting thought should have in inself considerable power of attraction for the will and thus for the attention. Accordingly, we must set up for ourselves favorite thoughts to which we resort when we wish to rid ourselves of unpleasant thoughts.

Conditioned Reactions. It is simpler to remove thoughts which are not colored by feelings of pleasure in themselves. The fear of blushing, becoming hoarse, or getting excited when lecturing, of having fainting spells, etc., produces these conditions again, as is known, if they have happened to us before and if we give place to this anxiety. There is no need for favorite thoughts to drive away anxieties. One must be filled with determination but without any energy in the momentary occupation. If it does not entirely occupy our consciousness, it is too familiar and we must resort to indifferent impression and perhaps analyze in all its details an object which we perceive. When we are not actually under the spell, it is well to be as indifferent as possible to the condition which we fear.

Some Ridiculous Misinformation. A famous Berlin surgeon, Privy Councilor Schleich, who was an authority in his special field of surgery but not quite so competent in psychology, has recommended as a cure of obsessions, formal training in diverting ideas. Dr. Schleich learned from an unexplained source, that the founder of the Jesuit Order, Ignatius Loyola, used a special means of training his disciples to acquire extraordinary will power. According to Dr. Schleich, Loyola sketched to the novice an imaginary sensual picture and ordered him to elaborate it to the smallest details until it stood tangibly plastic before his mind; then, Loyola forbade him under threats of most severe punishment to think again of the sensual picture and bound the novice in conscience to confess at once if this picture ever again appeared to his mind. The admirable will power of the Jesuits, so Schleich claimed, originated by this means. We would not repeat this silly story, by which the prominent surgeon made himself the laughingstock of the civilized world, if it had not been used in the widespread system of U. J. Kruse as advocated in his book, *I Will—I Can.* In certain circles, all critical ability seems to disappear when Catholic affairs are discussed. It seems superfluous, indeed, to state again that neither Ignatius nor his successors nor his disciples have ever practiced training of thought of this kind; neither training of thought by an imaginary sensual picture nor formal training of thought in general.[2] Jesuit asceticism, so far as the writer knows, is satisfied with that material training which results generally from scrupulous rejection of temptation. It is true that it could not be based on the psychological findings of the present time, but the instructions of the trustworthy spiritual leaders of Catholicism have always been in conformity with the spirit of modern psychology. No convulsive rejection of temptation is urged, but the calm

[2] Cf. *Stimmen der Zeit,* 90 (1916), p. 513 ff. *Jesuitismus und Militärismus,* by P. Lippert, S.J.

and determined passing to another trend of thought is recommended.

FORMAL TRAINING IN REJECTING THOUGHTS VALUELESS

It is evident from our previous psychological discussions that formal training in rejecting thoughts is rather valueless, and even harmful. Schleich and Kruse suggest that we first become familiar with an idea or acquire a most impressive experience, for example, that we see a theatrical performance and then forbid ourselves to think of it. If it be necessary to demonstrate to a man who has lost all control of his thoughts and all faith in such a control that rejection of thoughts is possible at all, this procedure might be undertaken for the sake of furnishing an example. It is, however, entirely valueless to make a practice of this, because such a practice offers neither motives for rejecting thoughts, nor is it the effective means to provide extensive and attractive thought complexes as the substitute for a thought which is to be suppressed. Simple direction of the attention, as an elementary act, seems not to be capable of training. On the other hand, to banish thoughts is a great effort for the individual who, in following the advice of Kruse, seeks escape in an energetic "No!" and does not know the true means of the control of thought. Therefore, harm, rather than an increase of will power, is to be expected from Schleich's and Kruse's plan of training.

SYSTEMS OF THOUGHT COMPLEXES LINKED TO TIME

Rather accustom yourself and your pupil to practice the *age quod agis*. Let the pupil recognize the value which lies in the real man who is always heart and soul for a thing. Let him learn how delightful it is to finish his work quickly and well by devoting himself to his school assignments and later giving himself entirely to play; let him learn what unsatisfactory pleasure and what vexatious torture there is in giving divided attention to both for hours, in play which is disturbed by thoughts of uncomplete work. Formal improvement will result from such constantly recurrent occupations as wholehearted work and undisturbed play. After a time there will be fewer distracting thoughts both at work and at play, not in consequence of the greater attention, but because play, work, and similar attitudes will form more or less closed complexes. These complexes will be linked together not because of increased ability of concentration, but on the basis of the laws of association which, until recently, have not been properly appreciated. Accordingly, it will be the task of thought education to create a series of such complexes: complexes of praying, working, playing, falling asleep, rising, and eating. Linking up the complexes to definite times, calm rejection of interferences, a uniform process of performing them (the latter holds good especially for going to sleep and for rising) but above all, keeping thoughts of valuable content in readiness so far as it is not a question of eating, falling asleep, and rising, will guard against all disturbing thoughts at this time. This will diminish the power of the disturbing thoughts also in the future, as they will languish because they are so rarely repeated.

KEEPING MOTIVES IN READINESS IN ADOLESCENCE

As danger periods, there remains only the times when

the child may fall into the habit of daydreaming. Such times are best filled by good reading which stimulates the imagination or by free play in which the child can be creatively active. If these periods were also filled by firmly fixed complexes, the dangers of daydreaming would be warded off, but the young boy or girl would most probably become a dry Philistine, devoid of all initiative. The growing child must have an opportunity to practice control over his thoughts. We can expect meager results from purely formal practice of such control. If the child receives vivid and interesting instruction, if it becomes accustomed to the *age quod agis,* to promptness in its duties as a pupil and as a child, it will have sufficient formal training in thought control. But all this training will not be sufficient, if it becomes acquainted during the formative years with stimuli of the imagination which until then were unknown to it. In such a situation, all training of attention and concentration (such as is usually recommended in books on the will), which the child has undergone, will be entirely useless. The reason is simple; the training detracts nothing from the attractive power of the sensually fascinating object and, on the other hand, provides no motive that can divert the child from the object. In order to give up something good, be it only a pseudo value, there must be an adequate motive. Training of thought control must, therefore, keep in readiness motives sufficient for these crises of adolescence.

Choice of Motives. At this point we must leave the formal consideration of our subject, which we have followed. For we tell the educator too much and at the same time too little, when we urge him to provide the child with sufficient motives. The whole secret lies in the choice of motives. If the educator wishes to experiment on the child with the choice of motives, the training of the will may be harmful rather than useful. Should he open the eyes of the child and unfold the whole mystery of mankind, and paint in a series of unrelieved pictures the final consequences of uncontrolled thoughts? That would perhaps be a sufficient motive, but the harm might be greater than the good. At any rate, the intellectual development of the child would not be natural. The child would be crushed before the youth and the adult would be fitted for the battle of life. The child should not be approached with stronger motives than necessary. Thus, we might begin from the idea that the weak dreamer never becomes a hero or a brave man. If this idea does not take, try one which can be unfolded gradually. In this situation the values taken from religion are most helpful. They are, in fact, progressively unfolding values; they can be presented at first merely in their externals; the will of the heavenly Father, His satisfaction with the pure, and the grace He gives them; His omniscience and justice; until finally, the whole divine plan for mankind is revealed to the mature man in both the biological and supernatural aspects, and the appreciation for manly self-control is imparted to him.

The Strength of the Determining Complex. In addition another very important formal circumstance in thought control must be pointed out. We have observed that a thought is the more powerful the greater the complex to which it belongs, the more concrete, and the more intuitive and compelling its representation. The diverting thought must be powerful in a proportionate degree. This is a requirement which can seldom be fulfilled. Therefore, it is an essential part of the technique of thought control to suppress thoughts, which are known from experience to be dangerous, immediately upon their arising, before they have brought up their reserves. For, as a rule, our thoughts develop from general schematic and unemotional contours. He who has a little thought control, is aware that he must use these early stages, when the thoughts still lack special attractions and when minor countermotives suffice, to turn away from them. But if they develop to their full concrete strength, so much so that they arouse organic sensations, there will be need of very strong motives to control them. The desire to listen, like Odysseus, to the song of the sirens is not right, as our will is not tied by fetters.

EXTERNAL ATTITUDE — ENERGY — CONCENTRATION

Special Exercises. Kruse, in his book on the will, mentioned in an earlier paragraph, attaches great value to a rigid attitude. He prescribes special gymnastic training. In particular, he requires the student to practice a fixed stare. He must first fix his eyes on a certain point as long as possible, then look firmly at the point of the nose of a portrait, and finally also use this so-called "middle glance" in viewing his ordinary surroundings. Besides, it is recommended that the learner use energetic speech and energetic gestures, forceful waving of the hand, while he pronounces the formula "I will."

Goal Must Have Truly Subjective Value. From our point of view, all these things appear to be trifles of very inferior value. If a person has a goal, for the attainment of which he is really enthusiastic, which, in other words, has a truly subjective value, he achieves it without a "fixed gaze," or "middle glance," and without commanding gestures. Certainly muscular effort is of no use to him. In fact, all these actions combined consume considerable nervous energy and really weaken him. Discouragement follows from inability to make a resolution in a delicate matter, particularly when, on the one hand, the man has repeated his mighty "I will" three or four times without effect, and, on the other hand, finds that the countervalues continue to hold him back. Quite naturally he becomes discouraged by the fruitlessness of his efforts, and regards himself as a naturally weak-willed man of whom nothing great should be expected.

External Exercise of Little Use. However, in considering this matter scientifically, let us be fair and search for the little good that may be found in such a practice. We have seen that a strong man, as a rule, has strong consciousness of the self and, therefore, places a higher value on everything that proceeds from himself. What he has once resolved to do, he may not yield to another will if only for the reason that it is his resolution. Poise, glance, and gesture act in the same way. They contribute a little to the increase of self-consciousness, and thus favor the execution of plans once determined upon, and lend encouragement to new decisions. But they cannot give strength of will in a moral sense, because they do not furnish sufficient motives for the moral struggle. In applying these facts to educational practice we may say: Educate by athletics and play in order that youth may acquire strength and a worthy demeanor, but do not go to excess, so that strength does not become rudeness, and self-confidence does not deteriorate into brutal disregard of others. Beyond this, all will training, such as "fixed gaze" and the like, is superfluous. On the other hand, if you encounter a timid individual who thinks he must hide everywhere, such training may be an easy beginning and a stimulus, but it will remain valueless, if it is not soon replaced by substantial motives.

Formal Training in Therapeutic Education. In dealing with the control of thought, in a previous paragraph, we spoke of the frequently recommended training for attention and concentration. This training does not immediately produce will power, nor enrich us with valuable motives. Therefore, it can be entirely omitted from the education of normal children. Instruction in and prompt discharge of domestic work, which for this very reason may not be eliminated from the training of youth, serve the main purpose of fixing habits. It is quite different in cases of therapeutic education. If one deals with an absent-minded child who cannot concentrate, formal training of the attention, first by way of play, may produce fixation of attention, and to a certain extent make it a habit. But here also, the essential point will be to impart to the child a real interest in the occupations necessary for school and for life. A certain joy of accomplishment can gradually develop from concentration exercises, but experiments in English schools prove that a very considerable length of time will be necessary to make such a habit effective in everyday life. We may have to reckon with training for more than a year, even if the child shows good will toward the task.

THE EXECUTION OF SPECIFIC RESOLUTIONS

Not Effective Training of Will. One of the most appealing means of will formation is the execution of specific resolutions. The working out of a correspondence course of instruction, or a somewhat difficult course of reading carried out by regularly repeated effort, and similar exercises, are frequently recommended as most effective means of training the will. We question the value of such exercises for the formation of a generally strong, or even an ethically strong will. He who is gifted with the rather intimate knowledge of human nature will find individuals who have learned several languages by the Toussaint-Langenscheidt method,[3] and thus have spent a few years in strenuous work, without having at the same time become heroes of will power. Yet it must be conceded that a number of very important motives of the will develop in the regular and faithful execution of such exercises.

Some Essential Conditions. For persons who have lost all confidence in their will power, the execution of limited achievements which at the start last a few and later several days, may serve to destroy their notion of vanished will power. But even normal persons gain not a little self-confidence by carrying out such resolutions. Success teaches them that very valuable results can be achieved, and most useful knowledge acquired, by a little effort. Thus, enduring work as such is developed into an important subjective value. The possibility of boasting of such success and achievement is of no little significance to all to whom the praise and esteem of others is of fundamental value. More-

[3] A well-known German correspondence course specializing in teaching foreign languages. — *Note by Translators.*

over. the prejudice against the great difficulty of learning disappears. Some will experience, by regular work of this kind, a very beneficial influence upon the rest of their lives and gain courage for further undertakings. Thus, by the execution of specific resolutions, a whole series of powerful motives can be gained for the formal aspect of our will and activity in general, provided that no start is made with tasks that are too long, that no useless things are undertaken, and that from the beginning a benevolent control is exerted. But one can at once see that such exercises may lead to a certain pedantry. Therefore, we must not insist that a definite portion of the work shall be done day after day without distinction; free days must intervene, so that the pupil may become accustomed to resume interrupted work and not permit himself to become too rigid in these complexes. In addition, neither teacher nor pupil must be left in doubt of the fact that such exercises do not guarantee to everyone all possible achievements of will. Untruthful promises which have the quality of advertisements do no little harm.

PRACTICE IN SELF-CONTROL

Self-Denial. By self-control is meant the refusal to fulfill one's own desires and wishes. For instance, in the morning I should like to sleep an hour longer and have a real desire for it, but I deny myself this wish, no matter how hard I find it to rise. Again, I see people gather in the street; I should like to know very much what is happening, but I dismiss this desire and go about my business. Ascetics have always distinguished between a necessary self-denial and a voluntary one. Whenever one's own striving is directed toward forbidden things, it must be suppressed. But frequently no obligation prevents my yielding to a momentary inclination. If I were strolling about aimlessly, I should miss nothing if I inquired about the cause of the gathering of people. Educators of the will had just such cases in mind when they recommended self-denial as a means of strengthening the will. What may be expected of such exercise?

As a Cure of Weakness. Let us disregard the cases in which denial of lawful inclinations is recommended for an entirely different reason, possibly from a spirit of penitence or of love, so that these little sacrifices bear the character of voluntary penance or of silent proofs of the love of God. There remain for discussion two further situations. The one is to be characterized as a spiritual cure of an existing weakness, the latter as a merely formal exercise. As an example of the former kind, suppose someone has the fault of curiosity which often causes him to neglect his duties. He is advised to resist his curiosity not only when it keeps him away from his duty, but also when he could indulge it without any disadvantages. What shall be said, from our point of view, if such a person fights the inclination to look into the show windows or to read the latest papers, by means of an opposite attitude? Indeed, we can hardly expect an increase of will power, but we may certainly hope for the development of useful motives and helpful dispositions.

Such a person will learn, first of all, that the loss of news, which might be acquired from a show window or a newspaper, does not mean a painful sacrifice and does no particular harm in his life. On the contrary, he will learn the positive value of concentration through which his work and his personal inner life will be far better than before. Thereby, the attitude of resignation will gain in value for him. Besides these motives, other useful dispositions and habits also will develop. Perhaps he will entirely forget to care appreciably for external things. But this would not be desirable; he would merely become an eccentric. We should, generally speaking, not insist overmuch on external habits because nothing valuable for character is gained by such a course. On this account, all hope of improvement lies again in the nature of the motive which stimulates an individual to overcome curiosity. Accordingly, one will say to himself: I will avoid all useless observation of my environment in order not to acquire that unworthy and unmanly attitude which tends to aimless diversion; but I will not forbid myself moderate circumspection. Yet, it is not desirable to be deceived by any illusion concerning the success of such self-education. Unless the curious person is careful not to habituate himself to an undesirably rigid disposition, everything new will hold a special fascination for him and will occasionally cause him to betray his weakness.

Formal Exercises in Self-Denial. There remains for consideration the purely formal exercise which has for its purpose the education of the will by means of a constant denial of all possible wishes — those originating in weakness, as well as those which are permissible.[4] We need hardly say that we do not expect a strengthening of the

[4] "Seek every hour resistances and obstacles on which you try out your strength, resist the small desires, and when an inclination arises, say with determination: 'Just for that I won't.'" *Willing, A Royal Art,* p. 247.

will from such an exercise. But if some strengthening of the will cannot result, there remains no reasonable motive for a like mode of behavior, at least on the part of the individual whom Divine Providence has not called to an extraordinary mission in life to be led along some difficult path.

Where such a divine vocation is lacking, it is impossible that either a valuable motive or an appropriate disposition can be developed to hold an individual to indiscriminate inhibition of impulses. On the contrary, there is great danger that the burden of such self-denial will become unbearable so that at some time when a necessary and wholesome self-denial must be made the individual will fail and suffer a corresponding loss. I am not speaking of things which never become realities. Particularly in the years of development, isolated statements of ascetics on the mortification of the flesh and self-denial are picked up in moments of religious enthusiasm, and are interpreted contrary to the intended meaning.

Values Corrected, Will Not Broken. In this connection, one more catchword should be explained. In the advice often given to parents and educators, these words recur: "The will of the child must be broken." In another form this sentence sounds more reasonable but is still capable of serious misuse: "The self-will of the child must be broken." I wonder how this self-will is conceived? The best possible interpretation is special will, a mischief-maker besides the good will. Accordingly, there is only one remedy for it: it must be destroyed; it must be broken. If we turn from the catchword to the psychological facts, we shall probably find that in the case of a self-willed child his own aims have acquired exaggerated values, probably, as a rule, owing to the fact that the child has been spoiled by his parents. I should certainly not release such a self-willed child from obedience to the will of the parents. Under certain circumstances, this obedience must be obtained even by force. But it must not be thought that "self-will" will be removed by such compulsion, for the will is not wrong, *its aims* are wrong. The appreciation of one's own wishes is, however, little changed by compulsory measures, and therefore self-will remains the same as before. It is rather the function of education that the pseudo-value of one's own aims be reduced to their just proportions. The child must learn that every wish is not necessarily carried out at once and unconditionally, and that occasionally a superior will may set aims for him which are objectively more valuable than his own. He must, of course, learn also that no superior will has the power of setting up purely arbitrary demand, that only necessity and love establish aims for him. Thus, not the will is to be broken, but the values are to be corrected. There is only one means of breaking a will, and that consists in the destruction of all the values of a human being. That would, indeed, be the hangman's job instead of the educator's work.

ENDURANCE IN SUFFERING

Not Will Power. "He who has not been punished is not educated," was a favorite saying of the Greeks. The Spartans saw a means of strengthening the will in the endurance of physical pain. Painful, physical punishment is often justified on such grounds. It is important that the educator understand this contention. We have already seen that the faculty of enduring pain is not identical with strength of will. Reports of witches' trials and the like often note a ready endurance of unbelievable pain, which cannot be understood as an exhibition of special will power of the victims, but which proceeds from their peculiar motives. The Spartans made real sport of the endurance of pain, and ambition was the strength-giving motive which sustained them. Similar tales are told of the earlier military schools in which the corporal's rod ruled by the pain which it inflicted. Moral heroes, men with strong wills for all tasks of life, were not educated by that method.

Motives for Suffering Important. But it may well be asked whether serviceable motives are not contained in the motto, "Suffering without complaint." First of all it must be said that physical pain in some form has a place in every human life. Pain serves everywhere as a counter-motive either in a preventive way or in an alluring way. One man is deterred by the thought of pain from striving after high aims which cannot be reached without physical exertions; another man is tempted by it to neglect the discharge of his duties toward God and his family. It is extremely important that the nonvalue attributed to suffering be deprived of its strength. That can very well be done by voluntary endurance of suffering, not without any sort of consideration, but only if attention is always directed to the formation of the necessary motive. One surely can endure necessary suffering, but in recognizing its greatest possible nonvalue, can direct all his desire and hope toward future enjoyment of a value. Such a person is not steeled against suffering by suffering. But he may become inspired with a contempt for suffering; or he may consider suffering in the light of a contest which he must win; or he may even associate with it a motive applicable to all suffering, as did the saints who were filled with the motive of penitence or sympathy for the Saviour. With these conceptions at his disposal, a man will be armed for later suffering. Otherwise not.

Use of Suffering in Education. Fundamentally, then, no objection can be made against the introduction of voluntary suffering into the educational scheme, provided that suffering goes hand in hand with the motive formation discussed. Nevertheless, on account of the danger of numerous errors and deviations, the model of Sparta has not been copied by educators. On the other hand, the unavoidable occasions of enduring hardships should be exploited pedagogically. Military service, which was formerly compulsory in Germany, afforded one of the best opportunities for the use of pain, even if it was not used by all soldiers for self-education. At present, educators have at their command in the struggle against effeminacy only athletics and the faithful discharge of duties in spite of physical indisposition.

Motive Formation Through Corporal Punishment. One will perhaps see in this a justification of corporal punishment even for older children. It is beyond the limits of this monograph to deal at all with the problem of corporal punishment, especially with the question of its value as a means of atoning for wrongdoing and of preventing wrongdoing. The words of Scripture must be respected. More important for our present purpose is the question of motive formation by means of corporal punishment. In early childhood, when experiences cannot as yet be well elaborated in thought, the unpleasant effect of such punishment may be associated strictly with the misbehavior and may rest its negative tone of feeling upon this mode of behavior. But as soon as the child develops his personal experiences by reflection, he will be compelled to follow very intricate processes of thinking in order to gain an ethical and later on a serviceable motive against a forbidden mode of behavior and in favor of a recommended mode of behavior. Injured pride, the consciousness of being wronged, etc., will only too often obstruct the path of thinking like impenetrable underbrush. In the whole range of educational influences, nothing seems to me more difficult than to gain a serviceable motive through corporal punishment.

Social Depreciation of Suffering. However, a far better means to depreciate suffering is available to the educators of earliest childhood. Very few mothers, aunts, and older sisters suspect the heavy obstacles they place in the way of the child when they bewail and sympathize with every little injury the child suffers. Even in the case of rather dangerous injuries, the child has no idea of the real facts. Most frequently he is occupied with the acuteness of the momentary pain, and still more often numbed by the shock. If the adults present hid anxiety and gave the child to understand how insignificant the pain really is, how he would grow big and strong by it, they would, indeed, render the child a great service of affection.

Summary. To summarize, this should be said: Among the means of training the will, there is not a single one which can be expected infallibly and directly to strengthen a disposition for the whole of life and all its tasks. All available means have a value only in so far as they keep motives in readiness. The more general these motives are, and the more intimately they are connected with later situations of life, the more valuable are these particular means. But, if the simultaneous development of the motive is omitted, all these means are worthless, even harmful, because they create the illusion of an educational achievement. Even in the case of careful cultivation of the motives, however, none of the enumerated means is, either alone or combined with the others, sufficient for universal will training.

III

SPECIFIC TASKS OF THE EDUCATION OF THE WILL

IN THE preceding chapter, we were occupied with the evaluation of individual means for the education of the will. We said that none are equal to the task of a general training of the will; that they can, however, probably serve as support of the most important means of education — the formation of motives. It is now necessary to show how these motives are to be formed for the specific tasks of education. At the same time, we shall appropriately distinguish two tasks, or rather two aims of education, a formal and a material training of the will.

FORMAL WILL FORMATION

Three Stages in Volition. Three stages can be distinguished in every complete process of volition: first, the acquisition of motives preceding the resolution — we might call it the accumulation of will power; second, the resolution or rather the choice; and third, the execution of the resolution. Each of these stages is susceptible to formal exercise and training.

A. THE ACQUISITION OF WILL POWER

First Years of Childhood. Undoubtedly the educator must make the main effort for the acquisition of will power. Presumably, the first years of childhood are those in which the fundamental values for moral conduct are created. At this stage, there can be no question of a formal exercise in acquiring motives.

The Teacher in School Instruction. In school instruction, the situation is different. Here, a double purpose can be achieved. The most important motives, corresponding to every age, must be inculcated in the child. The work, which is to be done by the children in the spirit of the school, consists pre-eminently in a purely inner activity: they have to experience the corresponding values. A certain normal exercise in gaining values is generally included in this frequent experience of motive values. In the first elaboration of the motives, the co-operation of the pupils might be at the most preparatory. The educator can inform himself by questions about the present motive reactions; furthermore, he can ascertain whether the thoughts requisite for the apprehension of the motive to be presented are comprehensible to the child. But then he should introduce the motive himself in his own presentation so that the children may experience it in a certain serious frame of mind. So long as the educator succeeds in captivating and interesting his pupils, the purely inner work of following the teacher in thought and emotion will be most effective.

Raising the Child's Present Level of Values. But the independent acquisition of motives by the children can and must be practiced formally at school. For this character education, instruction in religion and history offers, better than any other subjects, abundant opportunity. A saint, a hero, perhaps even a fictitious personality will serve. For instance, little Peter has to make a resolution. Have the children experience with him the preliminary history of this resolution. Now is the time for the resolution to be formed. What should the person in question say to himself? Of what should he think; from what should he take courage? Here the children can look for motives. It is a convenient opportunity for searching the range of values of the child and to learn on what level the motive formation ought to be kept lest the children should become precocious. That, of course, does not mean that the teacher must keep to the child's present level of values. On the contrary, it is his task to lift the children to a higher degree of values, not indefinitely, but to the next higher degree. Besides, let us recall again that the supplying of any motive does not settle the matter, but whenever permanent educational results are sought, a motive must be aimed for which very closely fits into the complex of the permanent motives.

Sources and Uses of Motive Power. We may formulate this instruction in the following way: certain sources of power in developing motives are available to all, and other sources are available only to some children. Thus, religious faith, firm ethical or social ideas are sources of motives for all; national feeling, family tradition, for example, are sources accessible only to certain individuals. The educator must know them exactly; he must have a firm conviction of the value and the power of these various kinds of motives. On the basis of this conviction, he must accustom his pupils to resort always to these sources in the case of important resolutions. But he should take good care not to appeal to the highest good of mankind for every trifle. It is true that in fulfilling even the least of one's obligations with an eye to the highest values, man attains the highest perfection. Even a child may be moved, in rare moments of enthusiasm, to undertake and accomplish things with the highest values in view. But the teacher will dull the children's sense of values if day after day he tries to restore peace and order in the classroom by an appeal to patriotism and the like, after having allowed class discipline to go to pieces by his own lack of skill.

B. THE FORMAL PROCESS OF MAKING RESOLUTIONS

Values Determine Choice. Every resolution may more or less be considered a choice: shall I, or shall I not? Decision comes freely and spontaneously, but always in accord with the values. We cannot resolve on anything except that which seems valuable to us in some respect. If the question is a choice proper, we are, as a rule, not led by the idea of making a capricious choice because it happens to please us so, but by the idea of seizing the (at least subjectively) more valuable of two available aims. The formal quality of a resolution is, therefore, practically dependent on the quality of the preceding test of values.

Hasty and Thorough Valuation. As was shown in the experiments of choice, the testing of values can be twofold. A value may be overlooked entirely, and then the valuation will often prove to be more superficial and will make the right appreciation more difficult, especially when, at first glance, elements of nonvalue appear. But the testing of values may also be analytical. A hasty evaluation will, therefore, always be a minor evaluation. The custom of thorough evaluation proves in general to be useful in life, especially, for the reason that one remains faithful only to the aims which one has accepted as true values.

Alternatives in a Choice. Very frequently, the resolution will carry with it a certain nonvalue. Values, which the one alternative offered, must be relinquished, or some disadvantage must be accepted in the chosen alternative. So it is indeed in the case of all resolutions of vital importance. Think, for example, of the choice of a vocation. The choice of a calling always makes a strong impression on sensitive minds and will not readily let them arrive at a decision. In such a case, it is important to develop the capacity for making a resolution. But what does this mean? We must not think of an inner nimbleness of the will which can be attained by frequent resolutions. Neither is the freedom of the will helpful here, for the irresolute person fails to arrive at a decision not for want of freedom, but because he does not want to accept the nonvalue which naturally lies in every choice; at times also because, without sufficient reason, he hopes later to gain a better insight into the relative values of the alternatives. Such a hesitant person can be helped only if supplementary values are added to the inner values of one of the alternatives. Supplementary motives of this sort may be found in such ideas as the following: what is subjectively best is the enemy of the good; rather do something imperfect, than do nothing at all; he who hesitates is lost, etc. However, special formal exercises cannot be recommended for use at school. The normal person has no propensity to hesitate, and youth in general must be held to the careful examination of values rather than to quick decisions.

Honecker's Experiments. Only morbidly hesitating persons can successfully undergo long training in arriving at resolutions. Resolutions, under conditions presented as real, may serve as models for arriving at resolutions. Such conditions were required in Honecker's experiments. The subjects of these experiments were addressed in the following manner: "Imagine that you are in position to carry out both of two proposed things. You will intelligently and seriously decide on one of the two things so that you will have no reason to repent. Suppose that the resolution implies the necessity of execution." Then two corresponding possibilities of resolution are presented to the subject of the experiment; e.g., taking a walk, or going to the movies.

Exercises Useful for Defective Children. In the education of defective children such exercises may be useful, if the patient has to account for his conduct, so that the educator is able to impart those supplementary values to him, which help him to make a resolution in the case of a hesitant comparison of values. But, as in all other instances, these exercises must not continue without relation to life, else they are linked to a complex from which the supplementary values do not reach over to the resolutions of life. Therefore, the patient should often render an account of the process of his practical resolutions. These opportunities are to be used for the hesitant mind in making a quick choice of any vital value.

Play and Athletics as Training. Group play and athletics in general are especially recommended as training of the faculty of resolution. It cannot be denied that both possess a certain significance in the training of the power of resolution. But psychologists are no longer of the opinion that the faculty of resolution is a distinct intellectual possession, or a sharply defined intellectual ability which, acquired in any field, may operate in any other. The modern conception substitutes adjustability for what was considered to be the permanent faculty. But adjustability acquired on the occasion, does not simply appear on every other occasion; it appears only if (1) the subsequent occasion resembles the first in its general features; (2) if there is a reproductive transition between the two; and (3) if no countermotives arise on the new occasion.

Gratification of Personality. If, however, play, work, and social life are three entirely separate complexes for the child, he may, say in football, show an excellent faculty of resolution, and be entirely irresolute when it is a question of carrying out tasks or of overcoming a difficulty in the solution of a problem or of completing a former class assignment. Or, he may be unable in social life to resolve to ask a favor or to apologize for a slight mistake, etc. Here, as everywhere else, the educator must realize that education is far more difficult in the light of contemporary psychology than it was in the opinion of those who held the older psychological views. We do not form inner faculties, but we do acquire adaptability and, above all, values. But a value remains barren if it is not lifted out of the isolated exercise, so that it becomes a value in itself and is associated with all the occasions in which it is to serve.

C. SUCCESSFUL ACTION

Reaching an Aim. The only thing which matters in life is success. It is all the same by what psychic (of course, ethically valuable) means the aim is reached, so long as it is reached. No matter how we educate the child, we may be satisfied if we enable him to reach a definite aim, even with relatively little effort. According to our present knowledge, it must appear very hazardous to secure the success of our action by a strong volition. Is there perhaps another safe way at our disposal?

Successful Action the Aim. Let us first set up successful action as the aim of the general training of the will. The directions to be followed will always be: make the successful action a subjective value for the pupil, and take care that his subjective value, whenever he needs it, appears before his mind.

However, if I intend to establish a relationship as a subjective value, then I must know exactly what this relationship implies, and whether it is simple or complex. To know this is of importance. For as soon as we have to deal with a composite mode of behavior, any educational effort may fail in consequence of the fact that one part of this relationship remains a subjective nonvalue to the pupil. Accordingly, I must analyze the successful action. What is necessary for that?

What Is Successful Action? Its basis is a proper choice. First, do not begin anything that has not been thought out from all aspects and recognized as possessing a permanent and relatively high value. This has been previously discussed. Second, he will be successful who starts the execution as soon as practicable after the choice. Thus, not the hasty start, but a decided and early beginning, is to be presented as of value to the child; hesitation and delay are to be discouraged as nonvalues. The general norms for the process of the creation of values have already been given. Let it be stressed here once more that the practice of starting as promptly as possible is an especially appropriate opportunity for forming values. Thus, tasks which are assigned not from one day to the next, but for a later term, would offer an opportunity of learning the value of an immediate start. Let the reader find out for himself how this should be worked out in detail. We repeat that the value of an immediate start is to be worked out as a general value, and not as one which is good for schoolwork. Thus, the connection between the present and the child's future life outside of school may not be neglected.

Heart and Soul in the Work. Third, to be heart and soul in the work, to employ the *age quod agis,* is a condition of successful action. There is ample opportunity at school to inculcate this particular value in the child. But it must not remain isolated, but rather be present as a general and, in particular, an important value for success in life.

Perseverance. Perseverance must be named in the fourth place. What is the use of thorough reflection, immediate start, absorption in the work, if it is given up after a short time. Thus, the completion of a task must become a general value. Instruction in manual work offers the finest opportunity for this. The biographies of persevering inventors like Zeppelin, or indomitable discoverers like Columbus, Sven Hedin, etc., furnish attractive material. But why do some people stop their well-begun undertakings? Difficulties, vexation, and painful effort frighten one; new aims allure another. Thus, disdain for difficulties is to be worked out as a general life value; difficulties are present in order to be overcome; difficulties prove that a thing which is sought has a value. A little of the spiteful "just for that very reason" does no harm, so long as it does not grow to be ingrained obstinacy. And then again an antidote is necessary against diversions! Diversions are siren's songs. He who listens to them has the path of his life strewn with ruins. As a boy, he begins. What on earth is not lying in the drawers of his table and cupboard: a wagon without wheels, the body of an incompleted airplane. He is a failure at the end of his life; he has been doing odd jobs, changing his work every month, without decent wages, whereas he had in his make-up the stuff of an inventor.

Other Elements to Be Made Life Values. Perhaps other features of successful action may be found. These must be singled out in the same way and held up to the children as life values. After the individual elements of successful action have been discussed and practiced, they must be applied in a practical way in combination with somewhat more difficult achievements. The project method and work in the manual-training shop and the home-economics laboratory are well adapted to overcome the difficulties of such children.

THE CONTENT OF THE TRAINING OF THE WILL

Special Virtues. The matters we have discussed so far are formal qualities of evaluation, choice, and action which occur in every act of will. We have not, however, taken into consideration the aims of the will. But education must not only lead toward successful action in general; it must also cultivate definite virtues. The special pedagogical theory of aims enumerates them. We are concerned here merely to show how these special virtues are to be inculcated in the child.

CULTIVATION OF SEPARATE VIRTUES

General Method. The general scheme of the guidance of the will remains always the same and is exactly as in the case of the formal qualities: make the particular virtue of high subjective value for the child, a permanent value of which he will become conscious at the right moment in later life.

Truthfulness. One single example might be given in passing. Before I may speak of the value of truthfulness, I must know exactly what truthfulness is: truthfulness as a mode of behavior, not as a permanent inclination. Very much depends on the clearness of the idea and a careful description of attitude for the evaluation of truthfulness. Truthfulness consists in speaking nothing which one knows to be untrue. It is far easier to present truthfulness according to this definition as a life value, than to teach that truthfulness implies the telling of everything we know or what any questioner would like to know. The various opportunities of telling an untruth are naturally not the same at the different stages of life. How a man can be tempted to tell an untruth regarding an inner experience will be intelligible only in the upper grades. Only rather mature children will understand how a person may be led to declare, in a thoughtless way, that he was delighted with a picture, or a concert, or a visit, whereas, in reality, he was left rather cold. Thus, instruction in the external attitude must also be added to the explanation of truthfulness. Many a person would often like to tell the truth if an appropriate form of expression were available to him. Therefore, such forms should be taught and made familiar to the children according to their ages.

Values in Truthfulness to the Child. The second task for the educator consists in the art of finding values. What objective values are found in truthfulness and what non-values in lies? A lie, even a well-meant lie, diminishes the security of human intercourse. It is a disregard of one's neighbor; for it compels him to take into account things which do not exist. It decreases, without reason, the exercise of common human right to master intellectually the world of facts. Of course, philosophical reasons such as these make but little impression upon children. Therefore, the serious effects of a lie on human relations is best illustrated by true examples taken from life; after this the shame and the disadvantage of a lie to the liar may be pointed out. On the other hand, the respect which the truthful man enjoys must be stressed, especially if he tells the truth at a disadvantage to himself. The inner completeness, directness, and harmony of the truthful man who walks along straight paths must be depicted, whereas the liar must be shown as a man who acts at least a double part and often contradicts himself. The attractiveness of truthfulness is again made effective in considering the noble character of Christ; particularly His simplicity, uprightness, His sincerity toward friends and enemies, in good and evil days. Truth is so precious to Him that He says of Himself: "I am the Truth."

Teaching the Values. In an analysis like the foregoing

we find the values which are accessible to the child. We must now endeavor to find points of contact in order to make these values available to the child. An incident from child life furnishes the material: the story of a children's game, in the course of which a pupil cheats his fellows, is told. The listening children must be led to describe in their own way the consequences and to pass judgment. These are the beginnings of evaluating a lie. From these childish values we go one step higher, perhaps to find a value which is taken from social life and which holds true also for adults. But we develop it only so far as it can be understood and appreciated by the children. Thereby we conform to the previously established norms according to which the acquired value must be applicable to later life, and may be widened and deepened by the child itself. No matter how vividly we portray the discomfitures of a liar or the evil done by him, no matter how strongly we utilize feeling, however within reasonable limits, the value idea proper must be emphasized and must be inculcated as a principle which henceforth is based on the child's own discernment.

Deeper Strata of Old Motives. Of course, the more impressive such a portrayal of social consequences of untruthfulness is, the narrower is the circle of lies to which it is applicable. Therefore, nonvalues are of little use in the process of the education for truthfulness, which must be accomplished at all costs. Accordingly, we must proceed to make use of the generally recognized values as opposed to the nonvalues, of which the religious values are the most intelligible; namely, the appeal to the will of God. But the value of truthfulness is of universal application. For this very reason, here as elsewhere, we must not be satisfied to struggle against mistakes. The basis on which the general and objective value of truthfulness rests has already been suggested. It is a question whether or not the children understand any of these values. In a general way, this can readily be ascertained: we tell the story of a child who did not wish to save himself by a lie from an embarrassing predicament, and ask the children to express their opinions. Here we readily learn at which points we can make contacts with the values of the children. Then we step from the childish values to the next higher level of general values, intelligible to the children. We need not fear that the children will become precocious because we initiate them into the life values of adults, so long as we are guided by the intelligence and co-operation of the children themselves. In moral instruction, or in the formation of the will, the spiral plan of instruction cannot be avoided. In moral education and will training we cannot teach a given virtue in a given grade, as, for example, we may teach the multiplication table in the third grade. Growing children require constantly new aspects of motives, not new kinds of motives, but deeper strata of the old motives.

The Motive From God's Will. Let us point to one more fact. From the discussion of instruction for truthfulness it is evident how valuable is the motive derived from God's will. This motive offers a reason, valid for all cases; it makes all subtleties superfluous; it can be shaped into a sufficient subjective value for all men; and finally, it is a value that grows with the child who can draw more deeply from it as time goes on. This is very true; but the danger is great that the educator will make this manner of motivation a mere routine. And since objectively there is no better motive, some teachers are likely to be inclined to believe that they may dispense with the inner and natural values, which are harder to work out. If the immediate and sole recourse to God's will is to suffice, at least three conditions must be fulfilled: first, God's will must become of extremely high subjective value to all children and must remain so in the future. Second, the thought of God must be ever present in their daily routine, at the time of the instruction and in later life. Third, later in life the children must advance through personal meditation from the exterior motive of the will of God to the inner and objective reasons for this divine will. But nobody will admit that these three conditions can be complied with universally. If a teacher, nevertheless, wishes to choose this plan, the result will be the typical "pious man" who is so frequently caricatured. Such an individual will prove faithful as a matter of habit in fulfilling his simple obligations. But the thought of God will not readily occur to him in the difficulties of everyday life, and, therefore, he will not worry about telling an occasional lie. He will be lacking in the inner motives to be gained from the thing itself. The person who has had a purely secular education will perhaps be quite different. In his youth he has perhaps learned to esteem truthfulness; every lie appears to him as a cowardice, as a submission to others. Or perhaps he is too brutally frank to lie. Accordingly, he gives the impression of a man of character and honor even though his other notions of values are so low that he appears pitiful when other demands are made on him. The educator of the will, accordingly, must not give up the inner, purely natural values, but must proceed from them as a starting point. They are to be supported by the external supernatural values until it is possible to rest the child's motives on a higher plane of value appreciation and until the inner supernatural values are reached. These values are the intentions of God with men as the ultimate source of all commandments.

The Corresponding Mode of Behavior. If the values are worked out in this manner, the corresponding mode of behavior must be taught and exercised. Opportunities must be presented — in the life of the pupil as well as in the life of the adult — in which truthfulness is demanded, and the temptation to be untruthful approaches. These opportunities are to be associated with the corresponding mode of behavior and the involved motives. And finally, care must be taken that the whole process — resolution, mode of behavior, and motive — be repeated several times so that they will be duly impressed upon the child and kept in readiness. There can be no objection if such virtues, as truthfulness, were made an aim for a month so that their practice becomes an object of special attention, at least once during a definite time. Above all, the opportunities which school life presents must be utilized; frankness with which a child admits a mistake must be recognized by the teacher and considered as the most wholesome expiation for the mistake. A skillful teacher can make his class enjoy sincerity as a real sport. If he fully avails himself of the opportunity to develop further motives which lie at the foundation of such behavior and direct them to the inner self by transforming them into generally valid values, he may be sure of a great pedagogical success. But he must not give way to illusions: though perfectly heroic truthfulness even in the face of punishment, certain in spite of sincerity, prevails in a class, the pupils are not yet molded into genuinely truthful persons. All their virtues stand and fall with their motives. Nevertheless, such behavior, even if it originates at the time in an insufficient motive, is not to be underrated. Action in the sense of a higher motive, the *faire comme si,* has the great advantage of offering an opportunity to learn the inner values and the external advantages of this particular behavior.

THE STRUGGLE AGAINST FAULTS

Avoiding Faults. A considerable part of our virtue consists in avoiding faults. But this must not lead us to direct our striving for virtue to a negative course, to avoiding faults. If this were the case, our life would lack the inner elevation as well as the happiness imparted by the consciousness of having created something lasting and positive. It is advisable that our active effort to attain a given virtue be paralleled by carefully controlled watchfulness for avoiding the corresponding vice.

Particular Faults, One at a Time. The first rule here is: *divide et impera!* Divide them, and you will rule! Only one specific fault is to be considered at a time. It would be asking too much to require a man who is in the habit of lying to correct this fault at once. He must aim, first, to overcome the habit of telling fully conscious lies. Then he may approach the task of avoiding the untruthful and incorrect statements due to inattention, haste, and loquaciousness; then, truthfulness in ordinary speech and in his bearing, and finally truthfulness in his thinking.

The Negative Particular Examination. In following this plan the corresponding motives must be pitted against every fault. The motives must be taken either from the value of the contrasting virtue, which has been offended, or they may be taken from the nonvalue of the fault and its consequences. The intention of avoiding the particular fault must spring from these motives. The manner of behavior necessary for the avoidance of the fault must be developed into a special resolution which comes to the aid of the general resolution. The resolutions, the mode of behavior, and the motive are then to be associated with the opportunities in life where the fault is easily committed. And finally, this resolution must be recalled at regular intervals so that it comes to mind when needed. All these rules automatically involve dependence of the motive-idea upon the memory, as previously explained.

It is of great significance for the success of this "negative particular examination," as we shall call it with St. Ignatius Loyola, that we gain an insight into possible progress. This corresponds to the following general psychological law: There is no progress in training, if we cannot gauge and control our achievements. Hence, it is advisable when we make our daily examination of conscience to record the number of these faults which occur at intervals. The numbers which are put down in this manner, of course, do not represent a degree of moral progress, but merely a measure of the success of our resolutions.

Benjamin Franklin's Plans. It is interesting to note that a man educated under entirely different conditions, Benjamin Franklin, suggested the same means of self-education. From his autobiography we quote the following: "I made a little book, in which I allotted a page for each of the virtues. I ruled each page with red ink, so as to have seven columns, one for each day of the week, marking each column with a letter for the day. I crossed these columns with thirteen red lines, marking the beginning of each line with the first letter of one of the virtues, on which line, and in its proper column, I might mark, by a little black spot, every fault I found upon examination to have been committed respecting that virtue upon the day. . . . I determined to give a week's strict attention to each of the virtues successively. . . . And conceiving God to be the fountain of wisdom, I thought it right and necessary to solicit His assistance for obtaining it; to this end I formed a little prayer, which was prefixed to my tables of examination, for daily use. . . . I was surprised to find myself so much fuller of faults than I had imagined; but I had the satisfaction of seeing them diminish. . . . I made so little progress in amendment, and had such frequent relapses, that I was almost ready to give up the attempt. . . . Something, that pretended to be reason, was every now and then suggesting to me that such extreme nicety as I exacted of myself might be a kind of foppery in morals. . . . But, on the whole, though I never arrived at the perfection I had been so ambitious of obtaining . . . yet I was, by endeavor, a better and happier man than I otherwise should have been if I had not attempted it. . . . It may be well my posterity should be informed that to this little artifice, with the blessing of God, their ancestor owed the constant felicity of his life."[1]

[1] Autobiography of Benjamin Franklin, pp. 97–102 (Riverside Edition).

THE STRUGGLE AGAINST BAD HABITS

Courage, a First Requisite. The first requirement for the struggle against deeply rooted bad habits is courage. Many a man has been completely discouraged in the struggle to reform himself by the realization that he is falling from one grave moral error into another, and by the thought that he has done irreparable injury to his body. It would certainly be unwise to represent the moral, hygienic, and social results of bad habits as insignificant, for the sake of encouraging such an individual. A dogmatic statement of a universally applicable method of advising in such a situation cannot be given here. Still this general suggestion can be made: The man who feels tempted to give up all hope should consult an expert, he should ask a physician to diagnose his bodily ills and weaknesses, and he should consult a qualified spiritual guide about the condition of his soul.

Sudden Conversions. Deeply rooted passion may die at one blow, when a great ideal is suddenly revealed and removes a man into a world in which the alluring language of the past is ineffective. Such instantaneous spiritual changes are reported in the lives of the saints, with a definitive loss of relish for forbidden pleasures. Similar complete revulsions are occasionally observed in nonreligious popular movements which carry a man along into a new life. It won't do, however, to hope for such sudden conversions in ordinary circumstances. The average man must seek to shake off the fetters of bad habits in the course of a systematic fight, and he will succeed if he exhibits even a small degree of serious good will.

Control Is Always Possible. We say "good" will, not "strong" will. The pretext of innate weakness of will, to hide a resolution not seriously meant, is impossible in our conception of volition to hide a resolution not seriously meant. There is no innate weak will. Every man can control his habits, so far as they imply moral shortcomings, if he cares even in the slightest to do so, and if his self-control means more to him than the satisfaction of his passions. That, of course, must be presupposed.

Overcoming Sensual Passions. Good will finds the first obstacle, which is not easily overcome, in one's own body. All the sensual passions, excesses, habits of pleasure, intoxicating poisons, sexual passions, etc., gradually produce changes in the organism, from which arise stimuli and needs of which the healthy man is either not aware at all, or only to a minor degree. For overcoming habits of using liquor, morphine, and the like, there are at present trustworthy medical cures, which gradually decrease the abnormal organic necessities. But these cures cannot do away with the simultaneous and subsequent moral struggles. In order to decrease sexual stimuli there are at present only general rules for strengthening the nerves. Of these the principal rules are:

"Do nothing that weakens the body and especially the nerves; take as little alcohol, nicotine, tea, coffee, etc., as possible.

"Do not sleep in too warm and too soft a bed; lie on the side, and not on the back when asleep.

"Eat moderately substantial and rather coarse food.

"Get plenty of exercise, work, and athletics in the open air, but avoid excessive fatigue.

"Avoid all sexually exciting reading and plays which produce the same effect."

Offensive the Best Defense in Psychic Struggles. This leads us to the consideration of the psychic struggle. Most important and most effective for this is positive work. It has been noted by statesmen that countries have often freed themselves from home troubles by conquering a neighboring state. An offensive is here also the best defensive; an offensive which is not directed immediately against the enemy, but which endeavors to conquer a new sphere for the mind. The finer and larger the sphere to be conquered, the more successful will be the struggle.

Vocations. For success in the psychic struggle, the high, inspiring, and momentous ideal of a vocation will serve magnificently as the sphere to be conquered. Later we shall discuss the ideal of a useful occupation. Such an ideal will furnish the ambitious imagination with ample material for its leisure hours; it will furnish serious preparatory work for a profession or other important occupation.

A young person's preparation for any of the important professions should not be limited by the necessary, prescribed studies. Many valuable aspects of a profession may become familiar to a student from a variety of sources. So simple a matter as reading the biographies and memoirs of the outstanding representatives of a profession will furnish much inspiration and help. Every profession requires certain professional virtues and skills, a certain ability to meet others without restraint, and a pleasing address which can hardly be acquired from the professional curriculum. Familiarity and to a certain extent practice in these will result from companionship with other young men of similar ambitions. Reflection and observation will reveal many a "prelude" to a vocation, which may provide both serious occupation and satisfaction.

Avocations as Playgrounds of Thought. He who has not yet found his ideal of a vocation must look for other congenial playgrounds for his thoughts and his imagination, as, for instance, special studies, music, manual work, gardening, nature study, social work, charitable activities, etc. At present, when youth is given so many opportunities of activity not possible in former days, it should not be difficult to find a hobby of some kind.

Sleep Time. If the whole day is thus filled with valuable, or at least interesting, work or amusement, temptation has, as a rule, only one breach through which it tries to enter: it is the time before falling asleep. (The habit of prompt rising at a fixed hour in the morning has closed the other breach.) But this breach can also be sealed. If one retires, whenever possible, at the same time, one very soon falls asleep by observing the following rules: at least for a half hour before retiring, nothing exciting should be read, and no intellectual work should be done. Then every evening a definite routine should be followed with utmost regularity; brief religious reading, evening prayer, undressing. Problems, memories, and systematic thinking should be avoided before falling asleep.

Unavoidable Occasions. In the case of a healthy person who is living a normal life sleep comes on of itself, induced by the chain of these associations. Thereby, the struggle against uncontrolled passions will be limited to a few unavoidable opportunities. I say unavoidable opportunities, for it is necessarily understood that all foreseen and avoidable opportunities will be shunned; that is the surest proof of a really sincere good will.

Temptation and Thought Control. And what of the moment of temptation? The underlying principles of the problem of meeting temptation have been discussed in the section on thought control. We suggest that it be read again. We have warned there against the energetic repulsion of a temptation. Instead, we advise that the attention be directed calmly but unconditionally and immediately to some favorite intellectual field which is usually placed beyond the possibility of temptation. In the case of a person imbued with religion, the thought of God's presence will arise of itself, and with this thought will also come the encouraging and gratifying thought that here is a precious opportunity, by a simple diversion, to give God a mark of love and faithfulness. On the other hand, the temptation will be strengthened, if one busies himself with it in any way, even if in prayer.

External Diversions. One more remark. One must gradually learn the ways in which temptation approaches. There is generally only a limited number of mental images with which the temptations are associated. If they are known and recognized on their appearance, serious good will as well as the skill of the fighter will be proved, by immediately directing attention into other channels. Such first sacrifices are easily made because the organism does not yet vibrate at this initial stage, and the temptation is, therefore, less alluring. But it is not as a rule sufficient to ward off a temptation only once. Mental images usually persist; i.e., they emerge again by themselves, especially when they – as is usual with sexual thoughts – are accompanied by organic sensations. Here help is found only in the repeated diversion of thought, insisted upon with the greatest calmness. Even the weakest person can succeed in this matter. If he calls to his aid external diversions — a book, a game, a bit of work — victory cannot fail him. I need not repeat here the religious aids, which may be resorted to at times when one is free of temptation: prayer, the reception of the sacraments, and the help of a spiritual guide. These cannot and are not intended to spare anyone in his struggles. Still, they facilitate to a very great extent, and often independently guarantee, the victorious outcome.

IV

WILL FORMATION AS A COMPLETE TASK

TIME *to Train the Whole Will.* If one may accept the findings of English educational research, it probably will require a year to make a vitally important mode of behavior a habit with children. In the experiments referred to, the attempt was made to teach children the habit of close observation, a skill against which only minor resistance arises out of innate inclinations. Let us now suppose that during one year every fitting opportunity has been used in school instruction to inculcate in the child the value of a definite, ethical mode of behavior, such as truthfulness, and that every opportunity has been carefully noted for practicing this virtue. We may certainly be satisfied with the results as such. But if we take into consideration how many moral modes of behavior and how many formal will activities are to be taught the child, we must despair of the possibility of making a program of adequate will training effective within eight or ten years of school instruction. Even if the family prepares the way for the school and later faithfully supports the efforts of the school, the prospect for the completion of such training of the will is very slight. It would not be surprising if many a teacher in the hope that the old psychological conceptions of will training are not altogether unfounded would forego the painful, systematic work of motivation and resolve to inspire his pupils to practice a given virtue, and again another virtue, as the occasion offers. Such a teacher would naturally hope that some of the inner acts of will and the outward discipline of the school with its opportunities of self-control might not be altogether unsuccessful in this direction. Fortunately, there is a way out of this difficulty.

Isolation and Relation. In its beginnings, experimental psychology necessarily occupied itself with single phenomena, and sought always to isolate and evaluate every phenomenon so far as possible. At present, more and more attention is given to the significance of the interrelations of phenomena. Indeed, the primary processes disclosed by psychological analysis are, in the first place, only creations of abstraction; to be sure, an abstraction which is based on the phenomenon. In exactly the same manner, will training will proceed, in spite of all attention to detail, from a whole and tend to a whole.

The Life Ideal. The solution of this difficult problem will consist in helping the child to reach his life ideal and to derive from this ideal the virtues and facilities which he needs for the realization of the ideal and of his life happiness. If we thus introduce the ideal, let us not discard the unifying thought which has constantly guided us so far. For the ideal is nothing less than a value, a motive; however, with this peculiarity that this value is a complete value, a complex motive in which all the motives required for the particular pupil are contained. The ideal is the most fittingly disposed motive because it contains a complex of thoughts, systematically yet concretely and, therefore, also emotionally adequate. The rightly comprehended ideal relieves the educator from the fear that he might overlook one or another vitally important mode of behavior in education. Rightly considered, it also secures the conscious presence of the motives at the right moment. That is why the most urgent question of the educator must be: "How do I impart the ideal to the pupil?"

THE SECRET OF THE IGNATIAN EXERCISES

"The Spiritual Exercises." It is a historically established fact that practically no mode of education has enjoyed such permanent success as the so-called "Spiritual Exercises of St. Ignatius Loyola." Any person who has undertaken the thirty days' exercises with good will, has come out a new man and has remained faithful to his new life aims with energy and enthusiasm. In view of such indisputable success, outsiders readily suspect some pedagogical trick, known only to the initiated. Even in our day, as mentioned before, a cultured surgeon has believed that Ignatius used coercive measures to impart to his disciples a marvelous control over their thoughts and, thereby, an astonishing firmness of will. This unfounded tale has been accepted by a recent journalist without any regard for the canons of historic criticism and has been incorporated in a widely used book on the training of the will.

Systematic Contemplation. It is true that some external means are mentioned in the "Exercises" of St. Ignatius, which are accessible to anyone in book form. Solitude and silence are recommended; the use of darkness and sunshine is mentioned; there are also suggestions for fasting and corporal self-chastisement. But all these are distinctly minor matters and, as suggested in the printed instruction, can be omitted according as they help the exercitant or not. They are all subordinate to the one aim, helping the progress of the meditations. The only means of the "Exercises," from which no dispensation is possible, and which admits of restriction or expansion only in measure and number, is the systematic meditation which constitutes the essence of the "Exercises." The task of the meditation is, however, the foundation of a life ideal with an objectively limitless value content and with the closest application to life; in other words, a central motive of the highest potency and the greatest closeness to personal consciousness. A somewhat detailed study of this spiritual edification and of its gradual acceptance by the exercitant will give us the best understanding for the greatest achievement of educational influence.

Their Basis in Personal Experience. The "Spiritual Exercises of St. Ignatius" are not the result of scientific considerations. Ignatius planned them before he began his philosophical studies. Neither were they concocted by someone who hoped to discover a most efficient means of influencing another person's will. Ignatius, on the contrary, outlined the "Exercises" according to his own personal experiences. His systematic, strictly logical, and thoroughly practical mind chose from the rich treasure of Catholic thought those considerations which had made the greatest impressions upon himself, and which he supposed would represent the most splendid life ideal, one which would permanently inspire all. His special merit is the systematic linking of these considerations and the fine and psychologically masterful direction in teaching them. We shall briefly outline the trend of thought in the "Exercises" in order to throw due light on the advantages of this pedagogical masterpiece and to reveal its entire secret.

The Central Value on the "Spiritual Exercises." The "Exercises" presuppose a faithful Catholic. They are not intended to serve as a way to faith, although the unity of the whole outlook upon the world which they convey, and their strengthening and happy effect on the exercitant, have often dispelled the last clouds of doubt. They begin with a rather sober philosophical consideration of this truth of faith: God is my beginning and end; therefore, the service of God is my task, and all that is found besides God, namely, creatures, can only be a means to reach the last end; creatures are to be used only so far as they serve this end; otherwise, they must be left unused. By this consideration, which may be developed further according to the mental capacity of the exercitant, the final aim, and thus the final value and final motive are given at once: one's own bliss in the possession of God, and accordingly the objectively highest value should be transformed into subjective value and become the end of human endeavor. In fact, this value was not introduced as something new, but was presupposed as existing in the living spiritual life of that time. That is why the introduction to the "Exercises" is brief. Ignatius supposes that the teaching of the home and of the Church have deeply instilled this value into the heart of the exercitant. At most, it might be somewhat hidden; therefore, a brief reminder should be sufficient to lift it into complete consciousness. Should it not be so, the master of the "Exercises" will find in the later meditations a model for making this value a subjective value. Ignatius should like to begin here also, as much as possible, from the "concrete" in order to paint more clearly the greatness of God and the happiness of the union with God. But he does not preach this idea to the exercitant; he presents it in a brief outline so that, as is stated in his book, the exercitant may find these ideas himself, which thus give him more pleasure and impress themselves upon him more effectively. This is the underlying principle of the present-day self-activity school. The director of the "Exercises" just hints at the way, but lets the exercitant make his own meditation.

The Associated Mode of Behavior. But in addition to the higher central value a general mode of behavior is also pointed out to the exercitant. It reads: Fulfill God's will, and use the things of this world only for this end, and prefer the better means to the lesser. The exercitant finds time in the long hours of meditation to look over his life in general from this highest point of vantage and to examine it on the basis of this norm; in other words, to associate this value and this general way of conduct with the details of his life.

Sin and Pseudo Value. Now follows a true estimate of the false value, sin, which is opposed to these resolutions. This is effected in the meditation on the punishment of God, in the consideration of personal sins, whereby the exercitant is required to penetrate the inner ugliness of sin. It is further effected in the meditation on eternal damnation. Indeed, the book of "Exercises," containing these meditations, pursues an immediately attainable end, such as the instantaneous break with grave sin by recognition, repentance, resolution, and confession. That is why in these meditations, as in no others, intuition and emotion are called upon to a high degree. But for later life, these sustaining ideas are driven home: "God is my end and happiness; the violation of the divine will is my greatest misfortune; sin is only a pseudo value." The ideas just stated engage attention of the exercitant during four or five of the thirty days' exercises. The meditations are repeated several times, especially the points which have made the deepest impression. During the time intervening between meditations, all distracting images and all religious thoughts not germane to the meditation of the moment, are to be avoided. However, between important divisions of the retreat, a rest day may be permitted so that the exercitant may relax by way of a long stroll.

The Two Aims of the First Week. This first week of the retreat has disclosed a central value and a central nonvalue, which are capable of constant subjective growth, and which display power enough for the most momentous resolutions as well as against the strongest temptations. That holds good especially for the nonvalue of hell. Nevertheless, the positive value, God's highest majesty and goodness, the happiness of the union with God, will rarely reach such a high degree of subjective value that it may now be considered an overwhelming motive for all vital decisions. Likewise, it will be clear to only a few of the exercitants how they must strive for this highest value; in other words, in what mode of behavior the service of God consists; for everybody has his special life task. The following three weeks of the "Exercises" serve these two aims, building up the highest value and finding the personal life ideal.

The Second Week. God's will, my life task and my happiness! This was the fundamental idea of the very first meditation on which the other reflections of the first week are based. It forms, as we might say psychologically, the anticipatory scheme, the external outline of the first week's thoughts which are connected to form a solid complex. This foundation is developed somewhat in greater detail in the beginning of the second week: God's will according to the example of the Saviour. God Incarnate (the Son of Man) is introduced under the symbol of a King sent by God, who is to free the world from the oppression of the heathen and the Turk, and who seeks to enlist followers in His army. The task of Christ is to free the world from sin and to make it happy by guiding it back to God. Who fights together with Him fights first against the evil in his own heart, then against his exterior enemies. Christ, the Leader, precedes us. He undergoes the greatest hardships just as any private, and endures even more. Victory, and the prize of victory are certain. Who follows? Ignatius appeals to generosity. Philistines should not enter this second week of the "Exercises" at all; they should be dismissed at once, after a good general confession and Communion, with some practical advice on the religious life. But he, who has a mind and a heart for the highest, will declare himself ready to follow the divine Leader as closely as possible. Of course, that is no longer entirely a matter of one's own resolution; one must be called by Jesus Himself to become a close follower. Therefore, this first reflection aims at the general resolution: "I follow Thee as closely as Thou permittest me to follow." The motives of this resolution are determined by the high task of redeeming the world. But these are not entirely new values; they are values of the first week: God, the aim and happiness of our life; sin, the only and true force of destruction. But these values have been brought into close contact with life: liberation of my own inner self from evil, and help for my neighbor. And the central value of God is to a certain extent envisaged (*veranschaulicht*) in the person of the Son of Man; *Apparuit gratia Dei Salvatoris nostri* (Tit. 2:11).

THE LIFE OF CHRIST AND A VOCATION

For about ten days after this, quiet meditations are made on the Incarnation, the birth, the hidden life, and the apostolical activity of the Saviour, always from the viewpoint that Christ seeks to lead man away from sin and to God. It is the task of the exercitant to watch for the call of God in these reflections; i.e., to observe whether he feels attracted to follow the example of the Saviour in one or other respect. In other words, he has to choose in these days the ideal of his vocation according to the model of the divine Leader. Not everyone is called to the same mode of life. On the other hand, there is no activity worthy of man, which could not be linked with the ideal of the Redeemer. Indeed, rightly viewed, every profession – the educator's, the physician's, the scholars, the mechanic's, etc. – has an inner meaning and value only in so far as it is modeled after the vocation of Jesus as Saviour. The little book of "Exercises" does not urge the exercitant along any special direction. The indication of points for reflection here become rather scarce, and the retreat master is forbidden in his occasional conferences to induce the exercitant to follow any particular occupation or profession. That is why many a one has taken up the "Exercises" with the idea of becoming a priest or joining an order, and has come away from them with the mature and religiously well-founded resolution of serving God as a layman. Only general directions, valid for all Christians, are provided in the book in the programlike reflections on the choice of a calling:

"Christ chose poverty and humility; the evil one on the other hand, urges to work for riches and honor." The exercitant is not forbidden by this to choose a life calling in which wealth and honors are to be expected; he must only be on his guard against being determined in his choice by a secret passion which plays into the hands of the evil one. In another meditation, he is urged not to be satisfied with half means, but to follow wholeheartedly any call of God which may reach him. A third reflection is not followed through to its final conclusion, but is proposed for consideration so that the exercitant may possibly grasp it: the deepest humility and the most incomparable following of the Saviour consist in the fact that in the person of the Saviour everything which happened to the divine Leader becomes dear to us. Just as a high-minded officer would dislike to appear on the battlefield in brilliant full-dress uniform while his king returns from the conflict blackened with grime and covered with blood, so the true disciple of Jesus will feel uncomfortable if humiliation and suffering are not his lot; nay, even if he were to choose, he would choose humiliation and the cross, though by this choice he could achieve no more than to become more like this Lord whom he loves passionately. Of course, let him, who can do so, grasp this thought. Let the exercitant just consider this, and if he does not yet feel he is strong enough for such heroism, he should at least pray that he may have a desire for it. He should make his definite resolutions in the state of mind; then he will not be led astray by pseudo values.

Respect for the Individual. Very remarkable is the respect which Ignatius shows here for the individual: Let everyone select from the abundance of the ideals embodied in Christ that which is in harmony with himself, without permitting any other person to give him rules or obtrusive advice. Merely basic directions are drawn up; naturally directions which, when followed, teach how to comprehend the ideal in its inmost essence; everything else is left to the candidate. This reserve was motivated for Ignatius by the supernatural conception which he had of the whole inner process of the choice of vocation: If the exercitant has discharged his duty, the Holy Ghost will take charge of the guidance of his soul; man has, therefore, to withdraw and must not interfere with the work of God. For this reason, he avoids also all exaggerated idealism. He does not preach: "You cannot choose your ideal high enough," but rather dampens the enthusiasm by remarking that a special call of grace belongs to a closer following of Christ. He seeks to arouse only the highest inner willingness in the pupil. And indeed, if this manner of expression were not open to misconstruction, the best advice to be given would be that the ideal be chosen as low as possible. An ideal is worthless which is sought for among the objectively highest values without a sufficient resonance in one's inmost self, else it will soon be abandoned. That is why Ignatius, in every reflection on the life of the Saviour, brings his disciple, as it were, close to the ideal and specifies as the purpose of the meditation in a general way more knowledge, deeper love, and closer following. He allows him to choose for himself in what respect and to what extent he will undertake to follow Christ.

Associating Future Life Situations. Whenever the exercitant has resolved upon imitating his divine Leader in one or other respect, he has also cast glances into the future in order to recognize on what occasion of later life the resolution he is about to make is likely to be carried out. Thus at least the most important events that can be foreseen are associated with the resolutions and with the motives for these resolutions. These motives are strengthened further in the third and fourth week, when the suffering and triumphant Saviour is the subject matter of the meditations. The deeper the exercitant has penetrated the spirit of the following of Christ in the second week, the richer are the motive powers which flow to him from these meditations of the third and fourth weeks.

Ideal Suited to Personality. The peculiarity of the "Exercises" consists accordingly in the fact that they lead the disciples to the independent creation of an ideal suited to their personality, not from abstract ideas, but from the "concrete" abundance of the characteristics of Jesus as they appear in the Christian world philosophy. This ideal is to be elaborated in such a manner that, with the happenings of life, it automatically rises to consciousness. Furthermore, it is basically conceived so that the most important modes of behavior ensue from themselves without the necessity of drilling and motivating every single virtue for itself; thus, conscientiousness, unselfishness, learning, determination, etc., flow from the ideal of a good physician, even if these qualities are not practiced and striven for individually. Finally, it is developed to such a thought complex, or better, into such a value complex that it may display at any moment all the values of all the "Exercises." A few more words on this.

Away From Sin, Back to God. The idea of value of eternal salvation and in the same sense, eternal damnation, is laid down around the central value of the foundation, "God is our goal." The thought and the value of the divine Saviour weave themselves concentrically around this. No matter how the Saviour is considered, He is always the One who will free us from sin and its consequences, and will lead us to God and His heaven. The values — God, hell, service of God, peace of the heart, etc. — are inseparably merged with the Saviour value. Then, the meditations on the Saviour's mission weave themselves concentrically around the person and office of the Saviour in all their details. The virtues of the Saviour unfold themselves. But every one of His actions is conceived merely as an act of salvation: Away from sin, back to God! Thus from every one of them, a radius leads directly back to the center. The exercitant forms his proper life ideal after this portrait of the Saviour. He may become what he wishes — a member of an order or a layman, a scholar or a laborer, or anything else that is suggested by his natural disposition. He cannot take up a fitting profession without becoming a fellow savior following the example of the Son of Man. Away from sin, back to God! Away from unhappiness, back to happiness! That must be the watchword of his life. And around the ideal image of Christ is concentrically laid the complex of the copy which is the personal ideal of the disciple. And all the motive powers for his ideal stream out of him from channels which, starting from the center, penetrate the whole system. He may, in case of need, call the entire motive complex to his aid: his personal ideal of a profession, the example of the Saviour, the effect of salvation, to be expected from this mode of action, his own happiness and that of his fellow men, finally God Himself, His fatherly kind will, but also His promises and His threats. Usually he does not need this recourse, but the strategy of great generals is realized here. All reserves are available for cases of unexpectedly great and violent resistance, and can be sent to the battlefield by the shortest possible route. If the exercitant has done his duty, he may safely assert that he has the strongest motives at hand against all temptations.

This Value Complex a Logical Connection of Motives. This is the way in which that wonderful value complex is developed. A few additional words about its structure. As already mentioned, it forms a strictly logical concatenation of motives. But this connection is arranged in such a way as to present a closed unity of two most significant formal qualities. Not one element of these motive complexes is isolated; a way leads from each one to every other, and especially to the central motive.

THE CENTRAL VALUES OF GOD AND ONE'S VOCATION

Thus, we can speak of two foci: the one is the central value of the idea of God, the other is the central value of the individual vocation. The whole arrangement of the spiritual edifice of the "Exercises" can be compared with a double cone, whose one point symbolizes the central value of God and the other the central value of the vocation. The one cone lies in the sphere of the divine, the other in the sphere of the human. If we imagine the surfaces of this double cone to be made of a system of cross wires, it will be impossible to touch any part of this elastic framework without the pressure spreading over the whole system. Thus, also the reflections and values of the "Exercises" are linked up with one another so that the total value complex is in readiness to act, and on stronger stimulation becomes conscious as soon as one of these parts is touched.

Furthermore, the circumference of this double cone is stretched in such a way that nothing could happen in the life of the exercitant that would not be caught by it. All events are anticipated, at least schematically, and have their places in the framework of the cone. Now, as to the second point: although the whole abundance and wealth of the central values spread out before the eyes of the exercitant, the permanent effect is not dependent upon those details always present to consciousness; they are comprehended in the simple and great ideas of the value of God and vocation.

System Capable of Development. There remains one last, formal element which deserves mention: the whole value system is of such a nature that it can be elaborated and deepened during the whole of life by contemplative reflection, and much more efficiently by experience proving the truth of those life values, which the exercitant has seen in the solitude of meditation.

Contemplation of Love. If the "Exercises" are well comprehended, the central value, the God value, will also be tremendously increased by meditations on the Saviour. To Him, at the end of the "Exercises," once more Ignatius directs everything. Of course, his suggestions for the final considerations on love are so sketchy that one must guess the connecting fundamental idea; that is why this reflection is often misunderstood and presented wrongly. It would be completely mistaken to see merely abstract speculations in these brief sentences. They rather breathe the spirit of true mysticism, which is, of course, based on a sure rational foundation. Therefore, no matter how deliberately reserved the instruction is, the internally mature person may find the connection by himself; the immature one, however, will not derive any benefit from this idea of value.

Let us briefly summarize the connection of the meditation on love with the preceding parts: what the exercitant has meditated upon and viewed so far is the great work of God for mankind. God, the point of departure and source of everything, should always have been in the foreground, and particularly when considering the work of the Saviour. But perhaps the immense value of God is not recognized by the exercitant and, therefore, it is well that the God-man introduce Himself as the mediator in this respect. But now, at the end of the thirty days, the disciple must once more view everything with reference to God. Perhaps God is now the great value to him, which places him at once on a higher level of life. What has this God not done for him! This is the point of departure of this meditation. The benefits personally received, of a natural and supernatural order, are to be gratefully considered, and the great work of creation, redemption, and eternal reward, which the exercitant viewed in the past few weeks, is to be surveyed once more. If the subjective conditions are present, an inner, glowing gratitude must be stirred, and all the emotions that have been gathered in the course of the preceding meditations are now alert and will vibrate with it. There is an urge of gratitude and return of love: "O Lord, take and receive all my freedom, my memory, my reason, and all my will, all that I have and own. Thou hast given me all this. O Lord, I return it to Thee. All is Thine: Dispose of it according to Thy will. Give me Thy love and Thy grace; for they suffice to me."

And this God, your benefactor, is not far from you. That is the second thought of the meditations. The omnipresence of God is not to be speculated on merely intellectually, but an awe-inspired feeling of the presence of God must be awakened. This sense of the presence of God can be experienced without interpreting entirely natural things as a direct contact with God. But the exercitant now knows whither his urge of grateful return of love is to be directed. There is even more: God does not silently and idly dwell in your closest neighborhood; no, it is He who works, lives, and labors around you and for you; the sun rays which warm you and make you happy do not glow alone and by themselves; it is your God who glows in them. The wheat in the field which grows day and night for your nourishment does not do so of its own accord; your God works in it for you. Thus, dry considerations on the *Concursus* are not to be established here either, but the concrete states of God's working and acting for us are to be actively comprehended. There shall not be anything on earth any longer in which the exercitant might not henceforth see his highest possession working for him with most faithful care. And if he thus sees everywhere these kindly, fatherly hands, he can picture to himself the greatness of this God by examining the value of all stages of beauty, goodness, and greatness in order to arrive finally at the infinite and personal God, and to explain anew his grateful amazement over God who is so great and yet so kind and who unswervingly serves him despite all his failings.

If the exercitant has reached that rare degree of spiritual maturity, he will suddenly perceive the whole experience of the "Exercises" in an entirely different light in the course of this meditation; this final meditation will make the whole panorama appear like an "Alpine glow." The exercitant will return to his profession an entirely different man. If he, nevertheless, has not reached this state of inward maturity, a remark in the book of the "Exercises" cautions him that true love consists less in sentiments than in action: the execution of his life resolutions will lead him then to the right way. But a part of those resolutions is also a definite life program and a daily program which gives him an opportunity to deepen and to revive those value complexes of the "Exercises," and to compare his life with his resolutions in a daily search, entirely aside from the purely supernatural means of prayer and the reception of the Sacraments to which the exercitant pledges himself.

Thus, the great secret of the effectiveness of the "Spiritual Exercises" is revealed: the inculcation of systematically arranged value complexes of the highest kind under the most favorable conditions; that is, an exclusive devotion to these thoughts and the universal connection of these value complexes and the resolutions motivated by them, with the opportunities of life; finally, securing them by the subsequent rule of life and habit.

COMPLETE EDUCATION IN THE FAMILY AND AT SCHOOL

Two Conditions to Be Fulfilled. The question arises whether this model of successfully influencing the will can be imitated in the family and at school. Let us first of all consider the question only in its formal aspect. Two conditions are to be fulfilled: there must be existent systematic and concentrically arranged value systems; and an individually adjusted ideal of personality must be gained from these value systems. Both conditions may undoubtedly be realized.

Different Value Complexes. There are many value complexes: the humanity idea, the national idea, art, science. And lastly, any occupation forms a certain complex of values. It will not be particularly difficult to arrange this concentrically. It is only a question what goal is set for the pupil, and whether the particular complex contains sufficient motives for the resolutions required by that goal. The question of the pedagogical goal is not discussed here. Therefore, we may point out only how important the examination of every value complex is as to its motive power. He who knows life will not in the least question the fact that the national idea is insufficient to motivate all the requirements of a moral life.

Not Multiplicity of Complexes, but Harmonious Integration. Therefore, one might get the idea that it is desirable to apply several value complexes, perhaps the morality value, the nationality value, etc. But this is not advisable for various reasons. First, this multiple value formation means an increase of educational work, as can easily be realized. Then the limitation of several value complexes diminishes their impetus. A man will be able to achieve very much more if his subordinated values also can receive motive power from the higher values. If, for example, the value of a good workman is isolated, it cannot yield the same energy as when it is harmoniously coordinated with the value of a good father of a family, of a good citizen, etc. But above all, it must be taken into account that our mental health cannot stand such a parallelism of complexes.

At present, we suffer too much from our inner many-sidedness, not to say, inner discord. Modern psychiatry has shown how often psychic weaknesses have grown into serious mental derangements, only because the patients did not work up their experiences into a satisfactory unit, but left them in a state of multiple disconnected complexes. Thus, if from no other point of view but that of mental health, it must be insisted that there be no multiplicity of complexes, but a harmonious integration and merging of the life ideals. Only thus do we form mentally healthy men of character and of internal solidity, who have at their disposal the whole force of their life ideals for every important decision, whether they have to make such decision as human beings, as citizens, as members of a profession, or in any other capacity.

Unified Life Ideal and the Denominational School. He who has understood the necessity of a unified life ideal will have no doubts on the current question whether the school should be secular or religious, denominational or interdenominational. His conclusion will be based upon the part which religion and denomination are to play in our lives. If denominational education is to achieve no more than familiarize us with the culture surrounding us as the outgrowth of denominational Christianity, if it is merely to provide our descendants with the bare understanding of religious ceremonies and pictures, and if it is to enable them to express some pious sentiment when occasion demands, then a school entirely without religion or an interdenominational school will suffice. And this school should offer as little instruction in religion as possible, the bare facts of religion, so long as it does not create religious or denominational complexes. If, however, religion and denomination are to be included in the life ideal of the children, especially if our faith is to be the central value of every life ideal, because we are convinced that it alone contains sufficient motive power for all the resolutions of life, then there will be only one solution of the education problem from the viewpoint of modern psychology, and that is, the parochial school. Such a school alone can harmoniously and concentrically co-ordinate the values which it teaches — especially the national and cultural values — with the higher life ideal. Through years of work, it alone can establish the associations between the requirements of everyday life and the motives and modes of behavior which ensue from the religious ideal. Denominational education in the family and religious indifference at school will, at best, form inwardly divided personalities. In less favorable situations, religious indifference in the school will certainly diminish, if not destroy, the religious ideals inculcated by the home and so deprive the child of all inner stability.

This fundamental position cannot be assailed by any consideration of the question whether parents shall be permitted to set up an ideal for their children before knowing whether the children will ever accept this ideal. It is sufficient that the parents are convinced of the value of this ideal so that they are morally obligated to acquaint their children with the life aim which has led them in their turn to happiness. This obligation upon the parents is parallel to that which obliges them to teach children those hygienic and sanitary practices and habits which they are convinced are right and necessary. On the other hand, it is not the province of parents and educators to prescribe for the child the personal ideal which he may find for himself in the great complex of objective values. Thus we arrive at the second condition, the acquisition of the ideal of personality.

The Ideal of Personality. To acquire a life ideal, as is provided through the "Exercises" of St. Ignatius, presupposes naturally rather advanced intellectual maturity. There may be some children who, as early as the time of completing the elementary school, have a general occupational ideal corresponding to their personal dispositions and inclinations. Whether they become watchmakers, painters, teachers, businessmen, etc., they overcome all difficulties and remain faithful to their early accepted vocational goals. But an occupation is not yet a life ideal. The ideal of personality has its origin in the way in which the occupation is conceived, and in the spirit with which it is permeated. However, such ideals are remote from the child's mind. And, therefore, the educator will hardly be able to present such an ideal to the children. Nevertheless, he need not entirely relinquish either a concentric arrangement of the ideal or goal of the ideal. After the example of the "Exercises," the central values and the concentrically disposed values can be formed; it will be left to the pupil to find his personal ideal as soon as he has reached sufficient maturity.

The Catholic Educational Ideal. Let us illustrate this by the example of the Catholic educational ideal. God as our Father, His holy will as the norm of our life, His greatness, but also His reward and His punishment, may become fundamental values to the child early in life. The example of the divine Child and the model of the good child may weave themselves concentrically around this base. It is sufficient that the child comprehends or suspects these complexes and their connections in dim outline. The most important virtues which are accepted from the very general ideal of the Child Jesus, such as obedience, diligence, piety, etc., may better be practical separately, even if the connection of the motivation with the whole complex must be cultivated. When the child grows older and has already an understanding of sin and virtue, the whole religious value complex must be developed in the course of the instruction in religion. So even at this time, in the so-called heroic period, the Boy Jesus must be depicted as one who achieves something — Jesus the hero. Unfortunately, this vigorous conception of the Middle Ages, as actually revived in the "Exercises," in the meditation on the kingdom of Christ, has been often eclipsed by mawkish portraits of the Saviour. The ideal of achievement which becomes apparent in the moral struggle should now be brought closer to the adolescent. No new objects of value are introduced here, but the value content of those which have long been familiar is developed further. Now again, individual virtues and formal faculties of will are to be utilized and practiced; the inner connection with the whole complex, however, must be developed much more strongly. The more mature the pupil becomes, the more distinctly are to be revealed to him the connections between world philosophy (*Weltanschauung*) and actual life, between the life goal and the personality ideal. Thus he is gradually to be led into selecting for himself such an individual ideal. The biographies of the saints and of other distinguished persons may present to him, now one, then another special value, and awaken in him that which is still dormant. Now consistent thinking on the basis of the ideal must be emphasized instead of a partial exercise of the virtues. The adolescent must learn always to draw independently the consequences which ensue from his ideal, for the individual situations of life. Then special training must begin for the modes of conduct which were still rather unsuccessful; in other words, especially salient faults are to be overcome in the manner described. But no positive virtue should be striven for alone and severed from its connection with the individual ideal. Perhaps the same idea caused St. Ignatius, the inventor of the strictly systematic and particular examination, to apply it to his own person during his entire life only in the negative form; i.e., to the successful struggle against faults, and not to the training in definite virtues.

THE LIMITS OF THE TRAINING OF THE WILL

Our conception, that everybody can become a hero of will if he only finds the corresponding subjectively valuable goals, appears to us more encouraging for educators and pupils than the conception that there is an innate will power that may be increased by training. For, some might too easily be convinced of their innate weakness of will and allow themselves to be deterred from any courageous resolution. Of course, there might remain the possibility of strengthening the will by training. But as the muscles cannot be strengthened in a case of innate heart and muscle weakness beyond a relatively low degree, just so little could be done with the will. Yet, even our conception must admit limits to the training of the will.

The whole capital of the will lies in the motives. But these are thought complexes by which we comprehend values. That implies two things. First, a more or less extensive complex of relations. Even here the factor of predisposition appears. Not all men can embrace the same range of conceptions which are the basis of the thoughts. It is true that for individual aims there is not always a need of a very extensive thought complex. A man who is driven by sensual passion can show unbelievable will power for such an isolated goal. But it is impossible to pursue a really valuable life goal, to act as a man of character in small and great things, without comprehensive trains of thought. For some, this will set the limit in the training of the will. Surely, many a comprehensive value complex has been thought out by others and has been reduced to a brief formula for their descendants. We may recall as examples the ideals of the founders of the great religious orders and the rules laid down by them. Such an ideal may be adopted by many a one whose glance never would have penetrated the distant horizon of the ideal which its author discovered. That person rears his will to higher ideals by another's range of thought. But his lack of talent will reveal itself as soon as new and unexpected tasks appear, which can be solved satisfactorily only by the original farsightedness of the founder. The narrow-minded, the petty, and the selfish person will here betray himself; for under the wide cloak of another man's ideal there hides, scarcely ever recognized and never really destroyed, a very narrow personal ideal: the satisfaction of petty desires.

Feeling and Value. Value thoughts like all other thoughts must proceed from a sense or concrete basis. I shall never arrive at a value concept without a value experience. This fact gives rise to two more conditions which regulate the growth of the values in every man: feeling and experience. The only concrete basis for the acquisition of the value concept is the feeling of pleasure; for only through this feeling do we comprehend what is valuable. Of course, there are individual differences also in our emotional predisposition. Hence, the value first experienced is not the same with all. From this it does not follow that the person capable of more feeling has also more will power. True, this conclusion does not sound altogether improbable if we consider how few saints have been produced by the cool North in comparison with the numbers who have come from the passionate South. Still, psychic conditions are never so simple. Momentous and attractive problems are here still awaiting experimental research. But the strength of feeling cannot simply be taken for a measure of the strength of will, for the simple reason that the real values of life are grasped by thought complexes, and vivid feeling obstructs the building of such complexes. That is why we often observe that women, owing to their more intense feelings, pursue practical, partial goals with astonishing energy, whereas it could hardly be asserted that we find as many women as men with farsighted life goals. But be that as it may, the capability for intense feeling is doubtless an auxiliary factor in the building of values, whose strength is determined by disposition; thereby the attainable strength of will also depends on innate predisposition.

Experience and Values. Our value formations are not confined to the immediately sensuous perceptions, but to their intuitive point of departure. Whenever we experience in our imagination a pleasurable sensation, it may become a new concrete basis for the comprehension of higher values. We may recall to the individual the happiness of his childhood, of the great pleasure he experienced in receiving the sacraments for the first time, in order to gain from such experiences an understanding for higher values. It is evident that all do not have the same experience. The day of First Communion of one person is recalled as a festival of the highest order because of a number of happy events: inner and external preparation, health and happiness in the family, fine weather, etc.—everything contributed to it. Another met with hindrances; the excitement was perhaps increased by troubles and quarrels in the family; the new suit or dress did not fit; there was, shortly before, a clash with the pastor; and the weather was as bad as the foregoing events. These two persons have had unlike value experiences on the day of their First Communion. If I wish to inspire both with a religious goal and seek to teach them the value of this aim, proceeding from the experience of the day of their First Communion, I shall fare poorly with the second. There are a number of such value experiences in life. One may assert boldly that there has been scarcely a man with extraordinary will power in whose life extraordinary events have not favored the formation of extraordinary values. But such experiences are not within our control. We cannot choose father and mother, the situation of the family, and other contemporary conditions, all of which have been instrumental in the formation of our values. True, we can acquire valuable but less effective experiences by enjoying nature, reading, art, the theater, travel, if our attention is called to them and the means for obtaining them are available — again conditions which are outside of our volition. Such experiences are not without significance for the formation of the will, and the person who is thrown entirely upon his own resources and is compelled to miss all these happy formative experiences will certainly not be ambitious for high-soaring resolutions. But all of the aforementioned things are mere trifles — makeshifts — in contrast with the really momentous, decisive experiences. And these we cannot create for ourselves. We have reached here the limits of the natural formation of the will.

The Need. It is in the province of a higher Power to grant such experiences. Hence, our theory of the will shows that we must expect as a grace, from the Hand which directs our life destinies, those effective experiences which lift us above ourselves. The natural formation of the will automatically passes over into the supernatural. Our faith makes us acquainted, in prayer and in the sacraments, with means of grace which, used to advantage, insure victory in the moral fight, without relieving us in the least of our own efforts. Of course, anything in excess of these gifts, necessary for winning the moral fight, we cannot obtain with infallible certainty even through the means of grace. That is left to God's free choice of grace. Using those natural and supernatural means most faithfully, we can merely place ourselves at the disposal of those extraordinary graces; but we must leave it to the Source of all graces whether we shall ever be numbered among the very great in the realm of those who are ever striving upward.

V

THE PRACTICE OF WILL FORMATION

PROBLEMS FOR GROUPS AND FOR SELF-EDUCATION

P. 30.

1. Single out the various modes of behavior required for the writing of letters, words, and sentences. To what extent are they entirely unknown to the beginner at school; to what extent are they partly known?

Compare the principal methods of instruction in the subject of writing with the theoretical discussion.

2. Reading, arithmetic, and singing.

3. The modes of behavior of decency, or good manners, etc.

P. 31.

4. The elimination of attention to the component movements in writing, drawing, and gymnastics.

5. The predominant considerations of the aim in the execution of greater undertakings.

P. 48.

6. Compare the conduct in the experiments of Ach, described in the text, with the most adequate conduct when translating into a foreign language (Latin), in games of skill, in discussions.

P. 63.

7. Observe your pupils and their environment with

respect to the manner in which they strive to make difficult resolutions.

8. Find the typically strong-willed children among the pupils. Where does their will power originate? Are they strong willed in all fields? How do they behave in other fields?

9. Make corresponding observations of the typically weak willed.

P. 67.

10. Where can the subjective values of the pupils be found?

11. What school tasks may the educator set to discover more easily and safely the subjective values of his pupils?

12. What values are rare, or cannot be found at all in the pupils? (Answers on the basis of your own observations.)

13. Find the values of the especially gifted and those of the backward children in the class. (According to your own observations.)

14. Compare educational (school) requirements and the actually effective countermotives.

P. 73.

15. Examine on the basis of the norms of motivation the well-known teaching methods of the cultivation of mental attitudes (catechesis, presentation of poems and of history).

16. Compare masterpieces of oratory with the norms of motivation.

Pp. 77–79.

17. Develop lesson plans on the introduction of certain values. Truthfulness, diligence, obedience, sociability, etc., must be experienced as more or less new values in certain

definite stages of life. The same for children with a pronounced trend of character. (Cf. p. 59.)

P. 84.

18. Find examples in the biographies of great personalities.

P. 87.

19. What exercises are performed by my pupils (or by myself)? What is their purpose? What motives have been cultivated so far? What motives can be cultivated?

P. 93.

20. What suggestions are conditioned by our present school life? What are their advantages and disadvantages?

P. 104.

21. How can education help thought control?

Pp. 107–110.

22. Teaching and educational plan on the *age quod agis*.

23. What guidance shall I give the child for reading and play in his leisure time?

Pp. 107–109.

24. (*a*) First, ask yourself: Have I ever succeeded in a task of rather long duration, a task whose completion was not due to the compulsion of external guidance (a course at school), but to my personal perseverance? If not, what test do I choose for myself?

(*b*) What achievement of perseverance may I propose to my pupils? How do I make it valuable to them? How do I gain permanent motives from such exercises for their later lives?

P. 118.

25. (*a*) Do I myself need a course in self-denial? In

what? The resolution must be renewed every morning; its execution must be checked by the daily examination of conscience.

(*b*) Are any faults apparent in my pupils which must be met with voluntary self-denial? How do I make the children understand this? How do I induce them to make voluntary the conscientious acts of self-denial required by the school routine? How long shall these exercises last? Practice lesson.

P. 121.

26. Teaching plan for a practice lesson on the preparation and presentation of a motive of different age grades.

P. 129.

27. Develop practical examples for independent motivation.

28. Play and athletics in my class and their pedagogical application to training the ability of making resolutions.

P. 132.

29. (*a*) Are there any more essential traits of successful action besides the ones named?

(*b*) Was my own action successful? Why did I not achieve success?

30. Make a detailed outline of an exercise in successful action (teaching and work plan).

P. 136.

31. Prepare a teaching plan for a practice lesson on the real meaning of truthfulness and its nature.

32. Prepare teaching and work plan on finding the value in truthfulness. (N.B. The teaching plan on the essence and nature of truthfulness must also indirectly cause the value of this virtue to be experienced in the teacher's high

subjective estimation which becomes evident from the whole treatment of the subject.)

Pp. 137–138.

33. Prepare a teaching plan for a practice lesson on the opportunities and mode of behavior for attaining truthfulness.

34. Prepare practical suggestions for the practice of truthfulness at school. Do likewise for the other virtues.

P. 139.

35. Teaching plan for practice lesson. Guidance for successful struggle against the principal fault (for higher classes).

36. (*a*) Have I already found my personal ideals? Does it give me instruction and motive power in all life situations? If not, the reason is that the ideal is wrong, or I have not thought it out sufficiently and have failed to connect it with my everyday life. Am I accustomed to think and act consistently with my ideal?

(*b*) Practical project of moral education in the elementary and the vocational school, in which education is to be regarded as a preparation of the personal ideal.

P. 166.

37. School instruction as well as the average home education has hitherto left the development of a personal ideal mostly to chance. Ask: Is it advisable to offer the adolescent special opportunities which are favorable to the conscious formation of, or at least the search for, a personal ideal? What could be done? At what age?

P. 171.

38. What motives are formed by prayer, by the

Sacrament of Penance, and by the reception of Holy Communion?

(N.B. According to the doctrine of the Church, the main value of the means of grace consists in their supernatural effect. Nevertheless, the motives naturally resulting from careful preparation and reverent reception of the sacraments must not be overlooked.)

INDEX